# EXPLORING SPOKANE'S PAST

## Tours to Historical Sites

Oldest Log Building in Spokane County

Photo by Clint Watk

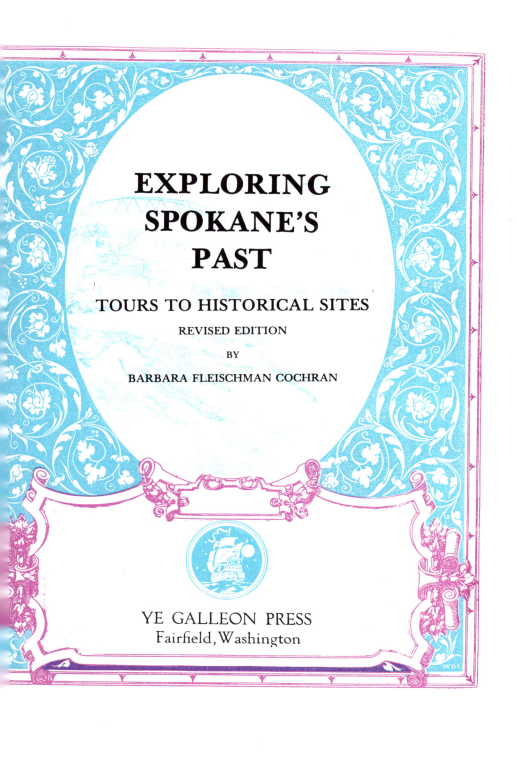

# EXPLORING SPOKANE'S PAST

## TOURS TO HISTORICAL SITES

### REVISED EDITION

BY

BARBARA FLEISCHMAN COCHRAN

YE GALLEON PRESS

Fairfield, Washington

**Library of Congress Cataloging in Publication Data**

Cochran, Barbara F.
    Exploring Spokane's past.

    Bibliography: p.
    1. Spokane (Wash.)—Description—Tours. I. Title.
F899.SC62                917.97 '370443              84-17285
ISBN 0-87770-337-X (pbk.)

# PREFACE

From the time of the Indians to the Fur Traders to Spokan Falls to the
etropolitan city, Spokane was and is a fascinating and delightful place to
e. Although not a Spokanite by birth, I have completely fallen in love
th this "my home" for more than thirty years.

This tour booklet probably doesn't include every historical site (so
any are long gone and no longer specifically definable) — perhaps it isn't
ssible to do so. However, I believe the major ones have been covered.
ads are straightened, property divided, buildings come tumbling down,
ing constant proof to the old maxim that "time marches on."
vertheless, directions for locating places are as up-to-date as one could
ake them.

Not intended as a complete history, sketches of events and places may
m too brief. Some tours perhaps encompass too much territory to be
vered in one day. No matter, you can do any in pieces or parts. This
oklet is only a guide which, hopefully, will pique your curiosity to delve
re deeply into the story of our area.

Good city, county, and state maps are handy. Don't forget your
mera, and HAPPY HISTORICALLING!

Barbara F. Cochran

**Painted Rocks**

# TABLE OF CONTENTS

JR                                                                    PAGE


Drumheller Spring—Spokane House .......................... 8
Kalispell Indian Caves—Little Falls .......................... 12
Treaty Tree—Plante's Ferry .............................. 17
Steptoe—Wright Battlegrounds .......................... 22
Cataldo Mission—Horse Slaughter Camp ..................... 27
Fort Spokane .................................... 32
Peaceful Valley—Fort Wright .............................. 33
Spokan Falls, a Downtown Walking Tour .................... 37
Spokane's "Age of Elegance" .............................. 49
A Conglomerate of Interesting Places ...................... 57
Epilogue: Trails and Old Roads .......................... 68
Bibliography ...................................... 75
Index ........................................... 76

Indicates those places listed in the Washington State Register of Historic
    Places.
Indicates those places listed in the National Register of Historic Places.

# Tour I

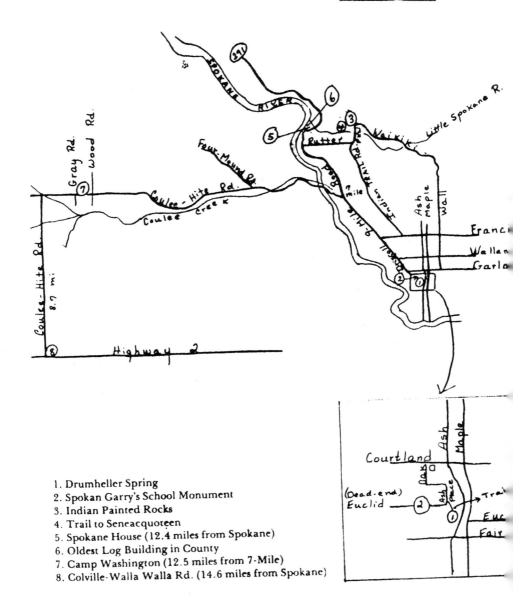

1. Drumheller Spring
2. Spokan Garry's School Monument
3. Indian Painted Rocks
4. Trail to Seneacquoteen
5. Spokane House (12.4 miles from Spokane)
6. Oldest Log Building in County
7. Camp Washington (12.5 miles from 7-Mile)
8. Colville-Walla Walla Rd. (14.6 miles from Spokane)

# TOUR I

## . DRUMHELLER SPRINGS *

The Indians had a trail from the falls on the Spokane River to the Spokane House
rading post. This spring was a stopping place along that route. Indian Trail Road in
orthwest Spokane is actually a section of that trail. Known as Spring Hill, this spring was
n important source of water for the early settlers as well as for the Indians.
ocated near Euclid Avenue just off N. Ash, a marker has been placed near the site. It can also be reached from
ie top of the hill on Ash Place. A trail to the spring is marked by two iron pipes in the ground.)

## . SPOKAN GARRY SCHOOL

Spokan Garry, youngest son of the Middle Spokan's Chief, Illim-Spokanee, was born
1 1811. At the age of 14 Garry was chosen by the Hudson's Bay Company to be educated
: the Red River Missionary School (near Winnipeg, Canada). Returning in 1831, he
arted the first school in the northwest in the Indian village across the river from the
bandoned Spokane House. The children learned simple agriculture, the Christian
:ligion, and to read and write. The confusion created by the conflict between the Catholic
id Protestant missionaries caused Garry to give up his public preaching and his school
bout 1840.

During the winter of 1870-1871, Garry conducted a religious revival among the
ookans and opened another school, this time near Drumheller Springs. When the Rev.
owley began a school for the Indians in January, 1875, Garry gave up his school and
eaching for a second time.
he marker for the second school is on top of the hill on West Euclid. See map inset.)

## INDIAN ROCK PAINTINGS *

Although the meaning of these pictographs are unknown, they remain a fascinating
nnection with earlier residents. The early Indians "painted" their pictures by crushing
d rock and mixing it with animal fat or fish oil. The resulting iron-oxide stain penetrated
to the pores of the rock making the drawings more or less permanent.
hey can be found just north of the Rutter Parkway bridge over the Little Spokane River.)

While here, take a look at **THE LITTLE SPOKANE RIVER**. This is the only
rviving stream in the State of Washington in its natural state. More than one hundred
ecies of birds, beaver, muskrats, heron, deer, ducks, trout and other fish call it home. A
iique heritage that we should cherish and protect.

## TRAIL TO SENEACQUOTEEN (pronounced Sin-i-a-ka-teen)

After the Hudson's Bay Company took over Spokane House, furs were transported to
nada primarily by waterways to the great fur rendezvous at Fort William on Lake
perior for shipment to England. (Prior to 1821 the traders traveled down the Columbia
ver to ship the fur pelts to China.) Some overland portages were necessary. One went
tween Spokane House and the Pend Oreille River. Following the Little Spokane River
st the Indian Painted Rocks, the route passed north of Mt. Spokane and crossed the
nd Oreille River at Laclede, Idaho. This old Indian ford was called Seneacquoteen, a
lispel word meaning 'crossing.'

In 1849 Alexander Ross, a Hudson's Bay Company employee, drew a map of the

Spokane Region and showed the portage to Sinny-acker-teen. Other early writings and maps show this crossing with various spellings: Syniakwateen (1866), Sinyakwideen Depot (1873) and Siniaquoteon Ferry (1881).

(South of the rock paintings is a pasture. On the west side of the pasture is a wide path along the north side of the Little Spokane River. This is part of the trail to the Seneacquoteen ford.)

## 5. SPOKANE HOUSE *, 1810-1826

In 1810 the North West Company, a Canadian firm, established a fur trading post at the apex formed by the Skichew (Spokane) and Spokane (Little) Rivers. At high water a slough between the two rivers creates an island of this land. The general area had long been a fishing and camping ground for the Middle Spokan Indians. Chief Illim Spokanee had a lodge near the trading post.

The fur trade was profitable, and competition was keen. As the Canadian-United States boundary had yet to be determined, both countries were interested in establishing claims to the area. It was not surprising when two years later the Pacific Fur Company, a rival American firm founded by John Jacob Astor, established a competing post a half mile from Spokane House, which was called Fort Spokane. The main buildings were of peeled logs and hand-hewn timbers. Wooden pegs were used in place of nails. The American post didn't last long, however. As a result of the War of 1812, the Americans gave up their post and the Canadians took over the buildings, leaving their island location. It is the outline of the American buildings that have been excavated and marked with colored posts. In 182 the North West Company merged with the Hudson's Bay Company.

Spokane House became the "Country Club" of the interior trading posts. The buildings were sturdy, the food good, the natives friendly; it was indeed a comfortable assignment. All of the wintering parties met here (except for the northern district) and were outfitted for the outbound journey. Unfortunately, the location was some six weeks travel out of the direct line for some groups, and "more or less inconvenient for all," wrote Alexander Ross. Finally, Spokane House was declared an unnecessary luxury by officers of the Hudson's Bay Company, and the post was moved to Fort Colvile near Kettle Falls in 1826. The buildings rapidly disappeared.

(Note: There are two spellings for Colville: one l refers to the Hudson's Bay post named for Andrew Colvile, a director of the fur company; two l's is the spelling for the military post (Tour II no. 3) and the city of Colville.)

It has been written, and rightly so, that "those were brave and daring times when our first citizens were a medley aggregation of canny Scots, volatile French Canadians, of Iroquois and Spokanes, of half-breeds and Sandwich Islanders (Hawaiians). Now and then a 'mountain man' from Kentucky showed up. French was the prevailing language spoken. Our mountains, lakes and rivers still ring with their names: Pend Oreille (earring), Coeur d'Alene (sharp hearted), Palouse (a grassy region), Nez Perce (pierced noses) and many others."

The Interpretive Center explains the development of the area and contains relics from Spokane House. It is open by appointment only, groups preferred. Call the Riverside State Park Ranger, (509) 456-3964.

(Spokane House is located off Nine Mile Road, State Route 291, 12.4 miles northwest of Spokane.)

## OLDEST LOG BUILDING IN SPOKANE COUNTY

Possibly built in the 1850s or 1860s, this building has been identified as the oldest log ructure still standing in Spokane County. Although it has no doors and the only windows en into the breezeway, the Indians used it to store their grain, hay and tools. However, it unlikely they built it as they never peeled logs. One can observe that the space between e logs is too wide for chinking, so obviously, the structure was not intended for people to ve in.

stands northwest of Spokane House and can be reached by the next road north of the Interpretive Center, or e can walk along the river to it.)

## CAMP WASHINGTON

Governor Isaac Stevens and Captain George B. McClellan were both assigned the task locating a pass through the Cascades for the Northern Pacific Railroad. From October to 30, 1853 their forces met at the forks of Coulee Creek where there was good water d an abundance of grass for the animals. At this camp Stevens made some of his first cisions as Washington Territory's first governor.

ne Camp Washington Monument is located approximately one mile north of the forks of the Coulee Creek on Coulee-Hite Road, 12½ miles west of the 7-Mile turn-off from the Nine Mile Road.)

The Gray Road (just east of the Camp Washington marker), a narrow, dirt road ding to the West Greenwood Cemetery, is part of the Colville-Walla Walla Road.

## COLVILLE-WALLA WALLA ROAD, 1811

This former Indian Trail became a main north-south route of travel, but came no ser to the falls on the Spokane River than fifteen miles west. A monument mmemorating the Explorers, Fur Traders, Missionaries, Soldiers and Pioneers who used s road was placed on Highway 2 where it intersects the old Colville-Walla Walla Road.

om Camp Washington follow the Coulee-Hite Road west, then south to Highway 2.)

Trail to Seneacquoteen

11

# Tour II

2 To Gardner Cave

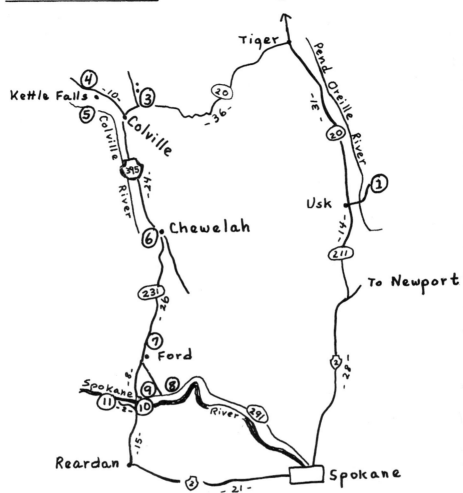

1. Kalispel Indian Caves
2. Gardner Cave, 12 miles, NW of Metaline.
3. Fort Colville and Pinkney City Sites
4. St. Paul's Mission and Ft. Colvile (fur trading post)
5. Meyers Falls
6. Old Indian Agency Building
7. Tshimakain Mission Site
8. Long Lake Pictographs
9. Long Lake Dam Viewpoint
10. LaPray Bridge Site
11. Little Falls

# TOUR II

## INDIAN CAVES *

Father Peter Jean DeSmet, a Jesuit Missionary among the Western natives, 40-1846, spent the winter of 1840-1841 with the Kalispels in the vicinity of Albeni Falls the Pend Oreille River. After wintering there, he followed the David Thompson-Finan cDonald route to the Kootenay River-Canal Flats portage to the source of the Columbia iver. It was probably during this sojourn that Father DeSmet named the largest of the ree caves, Manresa Grotto. A stone altar, wooden cross and rocks for seats have been aced in the Grotto for Easter Mass.

hese caves are on the side of a cliff along the LeClerc Highway in the Kalispel Indian Reservation, 5.8 miles rth of the bridge which crosses the Pend Oreille River at Usk, WA.)

## GARDNER CAVE

One night in 1900 as Ed Gardner was returning from his whiskey still just over the rder in Canada, his horse "spooked," throwing him. He landed in a cave, thus scovering the largest limestone cavern in the State of Washington. It is 15 million years d and has a slope length of 2000 feet. Rumors say Gardner kept his whiskey thereafter in e cave. In 1919 he lost the cave to W.H. Crawford in a poker game. Two years later rawford donated 40 acres with the cave to the State Parks.

rawford State Park is located on S.R. 62, 12 miles northwest of Metaline. The temperature inside the cave is und 45°, so take a warm jacket. It is open during the summer with guided tours on the hour, 9 a.m. to 6 p.m. charge. Picnic tables, restroom facilities, and fresh water are available.)

## PINKNEY CITY and FORT COLVILLE, * the Military Post, 1859-1882.

(About a mile before reaching Colville on State Route 20 from Tiger, take Aladdin Road (opposite a flying d) to the right to Mill Creek. Approximately 1½ miles one will come to a historical marker where Fort Colville s located.)

After the Wright campaign, the War Department decided a permanent military post as needed in the Spokane country. June 21, 1859 Major Pinkney Lougenbeel with four mpanies of the Ninth Infantry established Ft. Colville. It was an active post until Ft. okane, at the junction of the Spokane and Columbia Rivers, was built in 1880. In ptember of 1882 Fort Colville was abandoned.

Across Pine Creek a feeder town, **PINKNEY CITY**, sprang up to service the army st. That there were more saloons, including a brewery, than other kinds of businesses is t unlikely. It was named the county seat in May of 1860 for the newly created Spokane unty. After the demise of the fort, Pinkney City, too, faded away with most of the ople and businesses—including the buildings—moving to the newly platted (1883) town Colville.

## ST. PAUL'S MISSION *, 1845-1869

his mission is located on the bluff above the kettles of the Columbia River. The entrance road leading off U.S. is near the east end of the bridge over the Columbia.)

Following Father DeSmet's preaching to the Sxoielpi (Colville) Indians in August, 45, a small log chapel was built. Two years later the present hand-hewn log church placed it. (Restoration took place during the 1930s.) Sometime around 1869 St. Paul's ission was abandoned in favor of a location seven miles north of the present city of

Colville, St. Francis Regis Mission. (An Interpretative Center is being planned by the Sta Parks and Recreation Department at St. Paul's.)

## FT. COLVILE, 1826-1871, the Hudson's Bay Trading Post.

Named for Andrew Colvile, a director of the Hudson's Bay Company, this n trading post on the banks of the Columbia River below St. Paul's Mission was a relocati of Spokane House. When the backwater from Grand Coulee Dam flooded the origin site, the monument to Ft. Colvile was moved to the top of the bluff near the mission.

## 5. MEYERS FALLS

These picturesque falls on the Colville River near the town of Kettle Falls were the s of the earliest grist mills in the area. The North West Fur Company erected the first mi perhaps as early as 1816. The Goudy Mill of the Hudson's Bay Company replaced it 1843. To this mill came the missionares from Tshimakain and the Indians for a hundr miles around bringing their grain and returning with the precious flour.

L.W. Meyers built the third mill at this site in 1872. It is his name by which the fa are known.

(Located one mile south of Kettle Falls, these falls are now owned by Washington Water Power Company.)

## 6. OLD INDIAN AGENCY BUILDING †

Built of hewn logs in 1870, this is the only structure remaining on the origin Chewelah Indian Agency site. The Agency was created in 1873 to administer the Colvi Spokane and Coeur d'Alene Indian reservations. Since 1902 the building has be occupied as a private home.

(It is located two blocks south of the Museum in Chewelah at 309 Third Street East.)

Old Indian Agency Building

## 7. TSHIMAKAIN MISSION *, 1838-1847

The Reverend Cushing and Myra Eells and the Reverend Elkanah and M Richardson Walker established the first mission in the Spokane River Valley. The sit one-half mile north of Ford, WA, and about thirty miles south of Chewelah on State Route 231. Riding side-saddle all the way, these ladies were among the first six white women to cross the Rocky Mountains.

In addition to the washing, ironing and cooking over an open fire, Mary Walker also dipped candles, made soap, milked the cows, hoed the garden, churned butter, sewed, dried berries and pumpkins, pickled or salted down meat, and bore six children within nine years! She also taught her children to read and write.

After the Whitman Massacre in November, 1847, the Walkers and Eells went to Ft. Colvile. The next spring 60 soldiers were sent to escort them to the Willamette Valley. Unfortunately, no converts had been made among the Indians in the nine hard years at Tshimakain.

Later Rev. Eells returned to the Inland Empire. In 1859 he founded Whitman College in Walla Walla as a memorial to Dr. Whitman and organized seventeen churches in the Inland Empire.

(The Monument originally stood alongside the farm road—due east—which ran in front of the Mission buildings and was part of the Colville-Walla Walla Road. Erected in 1908, the monument was moved to this site September 10, 1938.)

# 8. LONG LAKE PICTOGRAPHS †

There are three separate paintings: two on a large rock near the road, and the third on the side of a cliff.

(From Ford, WA take the road toward Tum Tum. About .1 of a mile east of the junction with #291 are the Indian Paintings. The distance from Spokane House is 19.5 miles. The location is well marked and a parking area is available.)

Like other Indian rock paintings the origin, purpose and meaning of these are also unknown. One can only speculate. It has been suggested that the paintings were part of a young Indian's training in which he was required to spend several days alone in search of his guardian spirit. This was an extremely important part of his maturation. Since the guardian spirit usually appeared in the form of an animal, these paintings could have been an expression of the young Indian's vision.

These pictures and the immediate area were considered sacred by the Indians, and we, too, should treat them with respect.

## LONG LAKE CAMP and PICNIC AREA

(Just .2 of a mile west of the Pictographs is the entrance to this picnic and camping area overlooking Long Lake. Water and toilet facilities are available.)

At the picnic area is a sign giving us an insight into the lives of the Indians who inhabited this area.

Until the turn of the century (1900), Indians of this Plateau area lived in small family groups during the winter. These winter villages were ideally situated, located in ravines sheltered from the wind, with good sources of water, plants and firewood. In summer, families grouped together in large camps to harvest roots and salmon for the coming winter. These combined subsistence activities were important socially, religiously, and economically.

Camas, bitterroot and other plants comprised over 60% of the Indian diet. The Indians took advantage of the fact that edible roots were beneficially affected by controlled burning. They burned the root field twice a year to eliminate competition from other plants. Salmon were trapped in the rivers and provided the main source of animal protein.

## 9. LONG LAKE DAM VIEWPOINT

Continue west on #291 for 3.8 miles. On the south side of the road is a viewpoint overlooking Long Lake Dam.)

Built in 1915 by Washington Water Power, this dam is 170 feet high. At the time of construction, it was the highest spillway dam in the world.

## 10. LAPRAY BRIDGE, 1865-1915

Approximately 3½ miles upstream from Long Lake Dam, the first bridge crossed the Spokane River in 1865. It replaced the ferries servicing the Colville-Walla Walla Road. Although the location is now covered by the lake, it still staggers the imagination to visualize teams and wagons pulling up the grade out of this steep canyon.

In 1860 James Monaghan went to work for J.T. Bates on his ferry at this site. Although the Territorial Legislature authorized a bridge here, W.J. Terry and William Nix who had bought out Bates failed to build it. Monaghan and Nix then took up the authorization and completed the bridge in 1865. After buying out Nix, Monaghan sold to Joseph LaPray in 1867. The bridge, thereafter, was known as the LaPray Bridge, 30 miles west of Spokane. It vied with the Spokane Bridge eighteen miles east of Spokane Falls, as the only means of crossing the Spokane River until the Howard Street Bridge was built in 1881. It remained in service until the backwater from Long Lake Dam covered it.

## 11. LITTLE FALLS

(Just less than two miles from Long Lake Dam, south on #231 toward Reardan, is a small green highway sign indicating a west turn for the Little Falls Dam. A good, light bituminous road winds 2.6 miles down into the canyon.)

Little Falls Dam was built by Washington Water Power in 1910 and is located five miles downstream from Long Lake Dam.

Just in front (downstream) of the dam are the Little Falls of the Spokane River. (The city of Spokane is built around the Big or Great Falls of the river.) This was one of the most important salmon catching locations for the Indians. Each summer saw four salmon runs — each having a different kind of salmon. The Missionaries at Tshimakain also came here for food. In her diary Mary Richardson Walker said she saw more than 1000 Indians at a time at the Little Falls.

**Old Power Plant at Myers Falls**

# Tour III

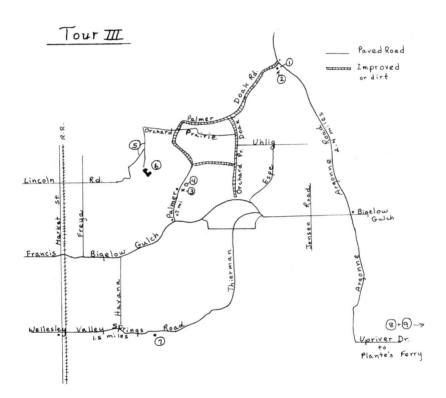

1. Treaty Tree
2. Original Site of St. Michael's Church
3. St. Michael's Mission Church
4. Old Indian Cemetery
5. Mt. St. Michael's Cemetery
6. St. Joseph's, formerly Mt. St. Michael's Scholasticate
7. Spokan Garry's Home Site
8. R.N. Riblet mansion and Point
9. Plante's Ferry Park

# TOUR III

## 1. TREATY TREE

Although it is not possible to document whether or not any treaties were actually signed here, legend has it that the Indians met Governor Isaac Stevens at this location in 1855. Under this tree which was cherished by the Indians, Chief Peone of the Upper Spokans and the early settlers supposedly smoked the peace pipe. A long-time resident of the area, Mr. Durheim says, *"The tree is deeded to the land, and the land is deeded to the tree."*

(The Treaty or Conference Tree is a majestic pine on Doak Road just west of Argonne Road, 2.4 miles north Bigelow Gulch. As a sentinel, it stands alone in a cultivated field overlooking Peone Prairie.)

**Treaty Tree, Peone Prairie**

## 2. ORIGINAL SITE OF ST. MICHAEL'S MISSION

At the brow of the hill behind the Treaty Tree, Father Joseph Cataldo built a mission church in 1864. It is said that when he first came, the Indians were too busy salmon fishing (yes, in the Spokane River) to listen to him. However, Chief Peone invited him to come back in November. Again Father returned, but this time the Indians were in Montana hunting buffalo. Chief Polatkan, former head chief of the Spokans, gave Father Cataldo permission to build a small cabin. It was quite primitive, being made of logs with only a dirt floor. The priest promised to take the cabin down in three months if the chiefs were not satisfied. When the time was up, the chiefs wanted the tiny chapel to remain. A new building replaced it two years later. In 1880 they moved this church to Palmer Road where it burned in 1908. Again it was rebuilt.

(Since Doak and Palmer Roads in this area are on a north slope, they can be quite muddy and slippery. Unless the ground has dried out well from the winter snow, it would be adviseable to return to Bigelow Gulch Road and approach Palmer Road from there.)

## 3. ST. MICHAEL'S MISSION

As time went by the mission church was used less and less and became a target for vandalism. In 1968 it was moved to the Ft. Wright College campus where it could be cared for. (See Tour VII, No. 10.) The monument on Palmer Road indicating where the little church had stood is surrounded by shrubbery; look sharply.

(This marker is on the east side of Palmer Road, .7 of a mile north of Bigelow Gulch Road.)

## . OLD INDIAN CEMETERY

Just to the north of the church location is an Indian Cemetery where Chief Peone is buried. His grave along the east fence is marked by an old wooden cross. The ground here as sunk in. The Indians were buried in a sitting position, which was the custom of the pokans. To the east beyond the little orchard the pagan Indians were buried. Four of ather Schoenberg's family are buried in this cemetery. (Rev. Wilfred Schoenberg, S.J. ith others was instrumental in developing the Museum of Native American Culture.) he large cross in the center of the cemetery was erected by a 4-H Club.

## . MT. ST. MICHAEL'S CEMETERY

Father Joseph Cataldo, 1836-1928, was interred here as are some of his Indian onverts. Father's grave is in the fourth row south of the large cross.

## . ST. JOSEPH'S

This imposing structure was built in 1915 for St. Michael's Scholasticate which had een housed on the top floor of Gonzaga University's Administration Building for fifteen ars. This site purchased in 1882 by Father Cataldo cost $2.60 per acre. After the school osed in 1970, the Jesuits sold the land (except the cemetery) to the Tridentine Latin Rite atholic Churches of the Inland Empire.

## . SPOKAN GARRY'S HOME SITE

he approximate location of Garry's farm is 1.5 miles east of Market Street on Valley Springs Road.)

Although Spokan Garry had improved this land by planting crops and building nces, a white man filed a homestead claim on it in 1887, and Garry was forced to leave. e then camped in Peaceful Valley near Hangman Creek. Taunted and treated with dicule, he was again driven away. His last few years were spent on a little flat of land near dian Canyon Creek. (See Tour VII, No. 5.) Garry's farm property was still in litigation the time of his death in 1892.

## R.N. RIBLET MANSION † and POINT

Sitting atop a 425 ' cliff overlooking the Spokane River, this home contained the very test in electrical conveniences when it was built in 1924. So novel was it that even a movie wsreel featured it in 1929, as did several magazine articles. It is built of native stone, ite stucco and red tile. For 32 years the only way to reach the mansion was *via* an ctric tramway operating on a 1600-foot cable across the river.

There is also an Indian legend about the point. An Indian maiden named Myrtle, it said, jumped off the cliff to avoid marrying a man she didn't want. Hence the name, yrtle's Peak.

he Riblet Mansion is clearly visible against the skyline as one drives east from Argonne Road on Upriver Drive.)

## PLANTE'S FERRY *

In the 1850s Antoine Plante, a French-Canadian with one-fourth Cree Indian blood, tled here along the Spokane River and built a ferry. It was a fairly simple device erated by cables and pulleys. Since it was the only means of crossing the Spokane River, : ferry was a lucrative business. The charge was three to four dollars for each wagon, fifty ts a person and fifteen cents for each animal.

With the advent of bridges across the river, the Mullan Road ceased using this crossing. As the ferry business became less profitable, Plante sold his holdings in 1876 and moved his family back to Montana.

(On Upriver Drive between Argonne and McDonald Roads, a lovely park commemorates the location of this early day ferry. The monument and ferry location are in the west end of the park.

From the parking space the southern approach to the ferry is easily recognized, being the break in the bushes along the riverbank downstream from the cement plant's waste pile. Now cross the swinging bridge. As you start up the wider path leading to the picnic shelter, a trail branches to the right. Follow this to the top of a bluff overlooking the river. Here one has an over-all picture of the northern landing of the ferry below on the left. The ferry road and Mullan route followed the ravine up toward the present shops.

The old wooden ferry post was replaced with a cement one, and can be found when the leaves are off the bushes. Unfortunately, a large bush completely surrounds it.

The map on the following page shows a narrow and sometimes rather steep trail from the end of the swinging bridge which skirts the bluff, or during low water one can walk along the riverbank. The best times for locating the northern approach to Plante's Ferry and Mullan's Road is in the fall or spring when there are no leaves or high grass and river is low.)

Downstream is a horseshoe-shaped area which was the easiest place between the Falls and Lake Coeur d'Alene to ford the Spokane River. This was a well-known Indian crossing and the scene of numerous Indian rendezvous.

**The Northern Post at Plante's Ferry**

# Plante's Ferry

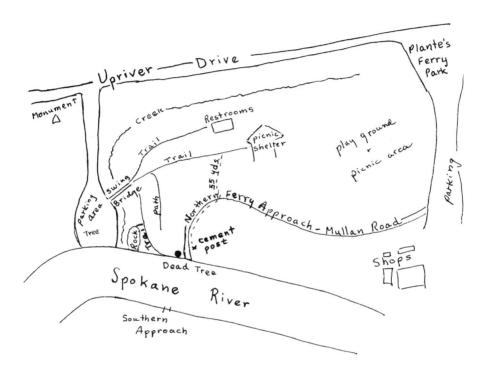

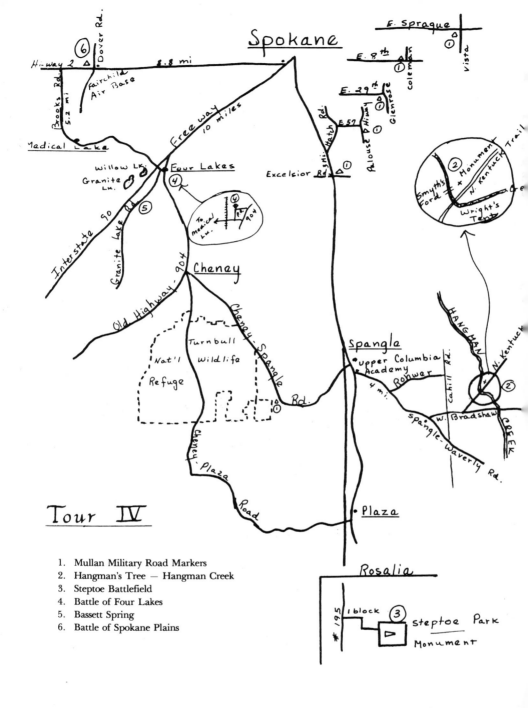

# Tour IV

1. Mullan Military Road Markers
2. Hangman's Tree — Hangman Creek
3. Steptoe Battlefield
4. Battle of Four Lakes
5. Bassett Spring
6. Battle of Spokane Plains

# TOUR IV

## 1. MULLAN ROAD, 1859-1862

Realizing the need for a military road from Fort Walla Walla, Washington Territory, to Fort Benton, Montana Territory (head of steamship navigation on the Missouri River) the U.S. Army assigned the task to Lt. John Mullan. After the Indian wars were over, work began in Walla Walla June 25, 1859. Mullan and his engineers labored over mountains, across streams and rivers, and through dense forests for 624 miles. The road crossed the Spokane River at Plante's Ferry until Schnebley's Bridge and Spokane Bridge were built. The road was completed August 1, 1862. (See Epilogue, No. 2)

Easily recognized remnants of the Mullan Road can be seen from the Inland Empire Highway 195 and at Plante's Ferry Park. (See Tour III, No. 9.) From the north-bound lane of #195, 1.2 miles from the monument on Excelsior Road, one can see several dirt roads below the highway to one's right. The road that angles northeastward into a grove of trees is the old Mullan Road. It winds down the hill to the banks of Hangman Creek. Several monuments are in the Spokane area indicating the route of travel: 8 miles south of Cheney on the Cheney-Spangle Road; 3 miles south of Hatch Road on #195 and Excelsior Road; on the Palouse Highway just south of 57th Avenue; on East 29th Avenue just west of Glenrose Road; on East 8th Avenue and Coleman Road; on East Sprague Avenue and Vista Road; and at Plante's Ferry Park on Upriver Drive.)

**Mullan Road from the Inland Empire Highway**

## 2. HANGMAN'S TREE, Latah Creek, September 24, 1858

Following the slaughter of the Indian ponies (see Tour V, No. 9), Colonel George Wright marched on to the Mission of the Sacred Heart (Cataldo). After settling with the Coeur d'Alene Indians, he sent word for the other tribes to meet him for a Council of

Surrender at Smyth's Ford on Nedwhauld (Latah) Creek. This was a well-known location and later became the crossing for the Kentuck Trail. One hundred seven chiefs and warriors representing the Spokans, the Colville, the Palouse, the Pend d'Oreilles and several smaller bands were present as the Council convened.

When the Upper Yakima Chief Owhi arrived, he was put in chains. Wright hoped to entice his son, Chief Qualchan, to surrender by sending him a message threatening the life of his father. Qualchan was wanted for actively leading sniping attacks against the white people from Seattle to Priest Rapids for three years. Although he never received the message, Qualchan, his wife, and a younger brother rode boldly and unsuspectingly into camp the next day. According to Wright's official report it was 9 a.m. and Qualchan was hung fifteen minutes later.

The following day six Palouse Indians met the same fate. Wright's justice was short and quick. Owhi lost his life ten days later while trying to escape at the Snake River. Since 1858 Nedwhauld or Latah Creek has been known as Hangman Creek.

(From the old Inland Empire Highway take the Spangle-Waverly Road just south of Spangle, passing the Upper Columbia Academy. Follow this for four miles. The second road one comes to on the left is North Kentuck Trail. Follow this for three miles where a sign directs one to a historical monument. There is space to park by the monument.)

Col. Wright camped on the flat on the south side of the creek, upstream from the monument. The actual hangman's tree is believed to have been cut down in the 1920s. It was located on the knoll between the old and new roads just east (in front) of the monument. The Indians reburied their dead in a scabrock area overlooking the canyon about half a mile eastward from the monument.

## 3. STEPTOE BATTLEFIELD †, May 17, 1858

The events leading to this confrontation really began three years earlier when the ambitious Governor Stevens attempted to force treaties with the Palouse, Spokan, Coeur d'Alene, Colville, Pend d'Oreille and other tribes, coercing them onto reservations. Although no treaties had been ratified by the U.S. Senate, the usually peaceful tribes were uneasy. Kamiakin, Chief of the Yakimas, traveled among the Indians agitating to prevent enactment of the treaties, and the rumblings north of the Snake River increased.

May 6, 1858, Col. Steptoe started out from Ft. Walla Walla on a friendly visit to the Colville area. Expecting a pleasant journey, little ammuntion was taken; sabers were left at the fort. The small arms of the men were out of date and of short range — no match for the long-barreled muskets of the Indians.

After several days of taunts and harrassment north of the Snake River, Col. Steptoe decided to return to Ft. Walla Walla. Ten hours of wild, confused fighting followed. It was impossible to meet the Indian charges while on the move, so Steptoe fought his way to the highest hill in the vicinity.

May 17, 1858, Col. Edward J. Steptoe and his force of 157 men received one of the worst defeats ever experienced by the regular army from the Indians. The site of the battle-field is in the area of Rosalia. A monument to the Nez Perce Christian Indians who led the expedition in a retreat under the cover of darkness stands in the hillside park in Rosalia.

## 3. STEPTOE BUTTE (This was **not** the site of the battle.)

Originally called Pyramid Peak, the name was changed to honor Col. Steptoe. In 1888 an elegant resort hotel with a powerful telescope was built on top of the butte by

**24**

James H. "Cashup" Davis. The story goes that he was called "Cashup" because he wouldn't give credit to anyone. A small community is named for him. Following Davis' death, the hotel burned. The site is now public land. A National Natural Landmark Plaque has been placed at the summit.

Steptoe Butte is a bald protrusion of 3,612 feet elevation consisting of older rock protruding through younger basalt flows. Similar geological features are now known as "steptoes."

## 4. BATTLE OF FOUR LAKES *, September 1, 1858

Following Steptoe's defeat, immediate reprisals were ordered. Col. George Wright was sent from Ft. Vancouver with 700 men. Leaving Ft. Walla Walla on the 7th of August, they crossed the Snake River on the 15th. By the 31st they had arrived at a spring one mile south of Granite Lake, having been followed by Indians for two days.

Sunrise of September 1st found the Indians assembled in large numbers on the hill southeast of Willow and Granite Lakes. (This hill is on the left with Willow and Granite Lakes on the right as one drives south on the Granite Lake Road to Bassett Spring or along the Freeway.) Shortly after 8 a.m. Wright advanced. Expecting the same kinds of weapons Col. Steptoe had, the Indians were driven away by the superior long-range rifle fire of Col. Wright's men. The battle lasted about six hours (until 2 p.m.) with no loss of army men or horses.

The "Battle of Four Lakes" monument is located in the town of Four Lakes, one block west of the Cheney Highway (old #904) and one block north of the Medical Lake-Four Lakes Road, kitty-corner across the intersection from the post office.)

## 5. BASSETT SPRING *

After the battle at Four Lakes, the army rested for three days at the spring where there was also plenty of grass for the horses and firewood.

In 1872 the Wilbur Fiske Bassett family homesteaded here, having come from Spokan Falls where Mr. Bassett had helped build the first sawmill. Their daughter, Minnie Maria (Ma-rye-a), was the first all-white child born in Spokan Falls, January 2, 1872. The family already had a two-year-old son, Herman Sherman.

Sadly, Minnie Maria drowned in the spring on the 19th of July, 1873, at the age of 1½ years. Bassett made a coffin, his wife lined it, and Minnie was buried on a little knoll about 400 yards south of the spring and cabin. Her father chiseled her initials, MMB, in a granite rock for a headstone. The grave and headstone are still there.

The youngest child of the family, Chester Wilbur, born in 1884, died at the age of six months. He was laid to rest beside Minnie. (Of the eight Bassett children, only three lived to adulthood.)

From Four Lakes take the Medical Lake-Four Lakes Road. Cross the railroad tracks and turn at the first left, Granite Lake Road. Continue south with Granite Lake and the freeway on your right. One mile south of the freeway rest area is the farm on which the spring and graves are located. This is ½ mile on a gravel road. The spring and grove of trees are behind the farm house on the east side of the road. The grave, like a tuft of grass, can be seen on the hillside just south.)

## BASSETT CABIN, 1874

After their first cabin burned, Bassett built another in 1874 near the spring. He sold in 1890. Ten years later the owner moved the cabin across the road to the barnyard.

Although an addition was added later to shelter cattle, one can see the solid dove-tailing of the corners and the hewn logs of which it was built. This little cabin is recognized as the oldest building in Spokane County built for a home that is still standing.

The big, red barn nearby took three years to build by hand, 1900-1903. It was made of hand-hewn timbers and wooden pegs. The water used for the cattle still comes from the spring: cold, clear and pure.

**Bassett Spring**
**Where Col. Wright camped in 1858, and Minnie Maria Bassett drowned at age 1½**

## 6. BATTLE OF SPOKANE PLAINS *, September 5, 1858

Marching north from Four Lakes, Col. Wright and the Indians clashed again. The fighting began just west of the entrance to Fairchild Air Force Base and continued eastward to the site of the future Fort George Wright on the Spokane River — a distance of fourteen miles. Hoping to bring their old guns within effective range under the cover of smoke, the Indians set several grass fires. However, Wright realized the danger and ordered his men through the ring of fire. Again their superior weapons won the day.

Of the 23 officers who took part in these battles with the Coeur d'Alene, Palouse and Spokan Indians, 17 subsequently became generals in the Civil War. Five of the enlisted men became majors in the regular army.

(The monument to the Battle of Spokane Plains is located on the north side of Sunset Highway — U.S. 2 — 8.8 miles west of Spokane in the northwest corner of the intersection of Brooks Road and #2.)

# TOUR V

## 1. TREATY ROCK

June 1, 1871, Frederick Post and Andrew Seltice, Chief of the Coeur d'Alenes, signed a treaty on the side of this granite bluff whereby Post bought the Spokane River channels and falls. It is said this is the only agreement in the United States made between an individual and an Indian Tribe written on a rock.

(From the I-90 Freeway eastbound, take Exit 5 into Post Falls which puts one on Spokane Street. **Note:** The westbound exit for Post Falls is #6, a mile east of Spokane Street. Turn south for one block. On the side of a building is a sign pointing west, "To the Falls." Turn *right*. At the "Y" keep to the right on the paved street. Park at the dead-end. There is a blacktopped path going under the freeway which leads to the Treaty Rock. A shelter with a wire window for viewing protects the painting. The distance along the walk is approximately two blocks.)

## POST FALLS

(Return to the "Y" and proceed on the dirt road west. After crossing a narrow bridge, the road turns to the left. A sign also points to the falls. At the end of the road by the dam is ample space for parking.)

This L-shaped dam controls the height of Lake Coeur d'Alene. A falls below the dam and the narrow river canyon provide a spectacular view.

The Spokane River at Post Falls consists of three channels, thus requiring three dams. You are at the Northern one. The middle dam contains the power house. All three dams are owned by Washington Water Power.

Along the south shore by the South Dam is a **CAVE** said to have been used by Frederick Post in 1871 when he was negotiating with Chief Seltice.

(To reach the South Dam, cross the river on Spokane Street. At the City Park turn right. Continue straight on this unimproved road; it will turn north. Park where it joins the road from the park. See map. Walk about 50 yards to the dam.)

Along the shoreline is a trail past the dam. Follow this as it goes over the rocks and downhill leading to the cave.

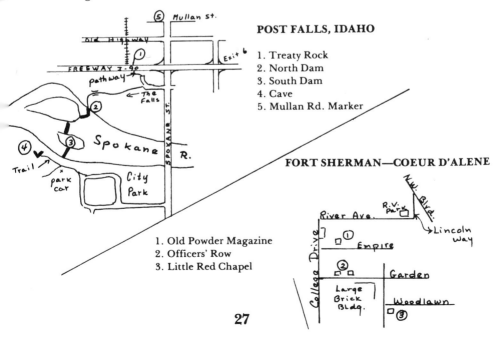

**POST FALLS, IDAHO**

1. Treaty Rock
2. North Dam
3. South Dam
4. Cave
5. Mullan Rd. Marker

**FORT SHERMAN—COEUR D'ALENE**

1. Old Powder Magazine
2. Officers' Row
3. Little Red Chapel

## MULLAN ROAD STATUE

At the intersection of Mullan and Spokane Streets, one block north of the O Highway, is a statue of John Mullan marking where the Mullan Military Road passe through Post Falls.

## 2. FORT SHERMAN, 1878-1901

Fort Coeur d'Alene was established in 1878 after the threat of the Nez Perce War th previous year. The location had been selected by the famous Civil War General, Willia Tecumseh Sherman. Nine years later the name was changed to honor Gen. Sherma when he retired from the army. The campus of North Idaho College now occupies the sit

(Take the first exit into Coeur d'Alene traveling east, Exit 11, Northwest Blvd. Angle right at the sign to Nor Idaho College. Turn right onto River Ave. at the R.V. Park.)

## OLD POWDER MAGAZINE, 1885

This small brick building, once a part of the fort, houses the Fort Museum which h early Idaho relics. It is open May 1-Sept. 30, Tues.-Sat.: 1-5 p.m. Downtown near t park at 115 N.W. Blvd. is the North Idaho Museum. Hours: April 1-Oct. 31, Tues.-Fr 11 a.m.-5 p.m.

## 1878 OFFICERS' HOMES

Two of these homes are still standing and in use by North Idaho College.

## LITTLE RED CHAPEL, 1880

The wood stove has been removed and the pews changed, but otherwise the Litt Red Chapel remains the same as when it was built as part of Ft. Coeur d'Alene. It was t first church and school for the early settlers as well as for the Fort. Located on Woodla and Hubbard, the Chapel is now serving as the Coeur d'Alene Christian Center.

## 3. STEAMBOATS ON LAKE COEUR D'ALENE, 1880-1938

The *Amelia Wheaton* commissioned by the government appeared in 1880 to ha hay and supplies to Fort Coeur d'Alene. Following the gold stampede more steambo: were built, the largest being the *Georgie Oakes* in 1891 of 160 feet. By 1908, 50 steam plied the lake. "*They brought ore from the mines; fish from the streams; timber from t forests; delivered mail and Sears & Roebuck packages to homesteads; carried cattle, wh and potatoes.*" They were also used for excursions; the *Idaho* could carry 1000 passenge Steamboats were once used more extensively on Coeur d'Alene than any other fresh or s water lake west of the Great Lakes. Each had its own distinctive whistle. By 1938 the l boats had passed into history.

## 4. OLD MISSION STATE PARK, 1848-1853

This historic mission is the oldest building in the State of Idaho. Located east Coeur d'Alene River, **CATALDO MISSION** † is easily visible from I-90 between Co d'Alene and Kellogg. No nails were available when Father Anthony Ravalli, a Jes missionary from Italy, went to work with a saw, an auger, an axe and an old jackpla With the help of the Coeur d'Alene Indians, timbers were cut by hand, and for mor they used mud mixed with straw. At one time over 300 Indians worked on the buildin Clustered around the church were a house for the priests, a storehouse, hospital, shop a a building for the use of the Indians.

In 1858 Col. George Wright met with the Coeur d'Alene Indians here and dictated the peace treaty. Generals Sherman and Sheridan also used the Mission as a place of rest for their troops.

(An Interpretive Center opened in 1979. Located 57 miles east of Spokane, the Mission is open year around. Picnic facilities are available.)

## 5. SIERRA MINE TOUR, WALLACE, IDAHO

The Sierra Silver Mine offers hour tours May through September: 9 a.m.-4 p.m., leaving every half-hour from the Wallace Mining Museum, 509 Bank Street. Fee charged for the tour. Pick up a walking tour of Wallace at the Museum. See May and Levi Hutton's home at 221 Pine, still occupied as a private home, and the August Paulsen home at 304 Cedar Street.

## 6. MULLAN TREE †

Two years after beginning the military road from Ft. Walla Walla to Ft. Benton, MT, Lt. Mullan and his engineers labored over the ridge of mountains between Coeur d'Alene and Cataldo Mission. As the 4th of July was a holiday, they rested under some pine trees beside a small creek. Someone, supposedly Lt. Mullan, blazed a white pine and carved the date: July 4, 1861. After the blaze was found, the canyon became known as the Fourth of July Canyon, and the tree as the Mullan Tree. Unfortunately, the top of the tree was blown down in November 1962 by a severe wind, but the stump still shows the carved date. A historical marker has been placed at the site.

(Since one cannot make a left turn from the highway, stop here on the return trip from Wallace. The turn-off is just before the summit of Fourth of July Pass and is clearly marked.)

## 7. M.M. COWLEY HOUSE, at Spokane Bridge, north of the river.

(Take Exit 299 off the Freeway. Take a right toward State Line Village, Idaho. After crossing the old bridge over the Spokane River, turn left at the first road onto East Wellesley.)

This old, two-story house sitting among the trees above the bank of the river was built during the 1880s by Michael M. Cowley (no relation to the Rev. Cowley). In 1887 he sold his holdings to Richard Lee Rotchford who ran the trading post at this location until 1908. Moving into Spokane, M.M. Cowley became a director of Trader's National Bank which merged with the Spokane and Eastern in the 1920s (now called Seattle-First National Bank). Cowley's home on Boone Avenue and Pearl Street was the first house east of Division Street on the north side of the river. He became a close friend of James Monaghan. When St. Aloysius Church on Boone Avenue was built, Cowley donated the marble altar rail.

## 8. SPOKANE BRIDGE, south of the river.

(Return toward freeway taking the gravel road to the right after crossing the old bridge. This brings one behind the Washington State Information Center and rest area.)

On the north bank of the river are concrete pillars which supported a steel bridge until 1950. This is the same location where the first bridge was placed in 1864 being near the headquarters of the Coeur d'Alene Indians. The approaches to the bridge on the north bank can be easily identified. This crossing was probably used by the Mullan Road until the railroad came through in 1883.

Clustered around the south approach to the toll bridge were some dozen log buildings including a store, hotel, dining room and post office. Spokane Bridge became quite an important community seven years before anyone lived downstream at Spokan Falls. Here the first post office in present-day Spokane County was established at Spokane Bridge February 26, 1867 with Timothy Lee as postmaster. When Mike Cowley bought the bridge in 1872, he opened a trading post on the north side of the river. His ledger book for 1873-1879 is in the Archives, Crosby Library at Gonzaga University. Cowley served as the postmaster from 1875 to 1879. This was an active post office until 1958.

Many an Indian swam his pony across the river to avoid paying the toll. To discourage competition, Cowley advised any prospective settlers to "go down to the falls and see what Glover has to offer" [after 1873].

(The **SPOKANE BRIDGE MONUMENT** is on the grounds of the Washington State Information Center.)

## 9. HORSE SLAUGHTER CAMP *

(Stop at the west end of the Highway Weigh Station before re-entering the Freeway for this monument.)

After resting his men a few days at the later-to-be Fort George Wright location west of the falls, Colonel Wright continued in pursuit of the Indians up the Spokane Valley. Whenever an Indian storehouse filled with their winter supply of wheat, oats, vegetables, camas roots, or dried berries was found, it was burned. The date was September 9, 1858. Near Liberty Lake the soldiers caught up with a herd of 800 horses being driven, hopefully, out of Wright's reach. The Colonel ordered the horses captured. Approximately a hundred were kept for army use — the rest were shot! The destruction of their ponies which represented wealth to the Indians as well as transportation, completely broke their spirit to resist any further.

As late as 1911 the bleached bones of the slaughtered horses could still be seen along the bank of the Spokane River.

(One and a half miles from the Idaho border between the Freeway I-90 and the Spokane River is a long, flat area. The west end and part of the south side are banked, forming a natural bowl in which Wright's men could easily have kept the Indian horses corralled with a barrier thrown up along the east end. The mileage sign: Spokane 15 is about center of the area. From the fence there one can see the Horse Slaughter corral below.)

**Horse Slaughter Camp**

IN 1858 COL. GEORGE WRIGHT
WITH 700 SOLDIERS WAS SENT
FROM WALLA WALLA TO SUPPRESS
AN INDIAN OUTBREAK. AFTER
DEFEATING THE INDIANS IN TWO
BATTLES HE CAPTURED 800
INDIAN HORSES. TO PREVENT
THE INDIANS FROM WAGING
FURTHER WARFARE HE KILLED
THE HORSES ON THE BANK OF
THE RIVER DIRECTLY NORTH
OF THIS MONUMENT.

ERECTED A.D. 1946
BY THE SPOKANE COUNTY PIONEER SOCIETY,
ASSISTED BY
SONS AND DAUGHTERS OF PIONEERS
OF WASHINGTON
AND LOYAL CITIZENS.

Courtesy Eastern Washington State Historical Society

This commemorative monument is located at the
Washington State Patrol Weigh Station on I-90 near the Idaho border.

# TOUR VI

## 1. FORT SPOKANE *, 1880-1898

In 1880 the Army decided to establish a post at a central location that would serve two purposes: to protect the settlers of the Upper Columbia and to keep an eye on the Indian reservations. Here where the Spokane River joins the Columbia River was the place which met those requirements. For eighteen years the soldiers enjoyed routine garrison life as the Indians were peaceful and the settlers needed little protection.

When the Spanish-American War broke out the entire garrison: men, equipment and furnishings were moved by wagon to the newly established Fort George Wright near Spokane.

Fort Spokane was transferred to the national Park Service in 1960. Only four of the more than 45 buildings remain:

| | | | |
|---|---|---|---|
| Quartermaster's Stable | 1884 | Reservoir | 1889 |
| Powder Magazine Building | 1888 | Guard House | 1892 |

The brick Guard House has been converted into a Visitor Center which is open daily, year around. Hours: May to Approx. September 15: 8 a.m. to 6 p.m.; Winter Hours: September 15 to May 10: 9 a.m. to 4 p.m. A ten-minute slide show in the Visitor Center tells the story of the fort. One can also step into a solitary confinement cell used when the fort was active. There is an interesting self-guided walking tour among the many excavated foundations of former fort buildings.

(To reach Fort Spokane take Highway 2 west of Spokane to Davenport [32 miles], then north on Highway 25 [24 miles].)

## LINCOLN COUNTY HISTORICAL MUSEUM IN DAVENPORT, WA.

This excellent museum of pioneer artifacts is open from May 1st until Labor Day, Tuesdays to Sundays: 1-4 p.m. There is no charge although donations are appreciated. It is located at 7th and Park Streets, just south of the main street. Directions are well marked.

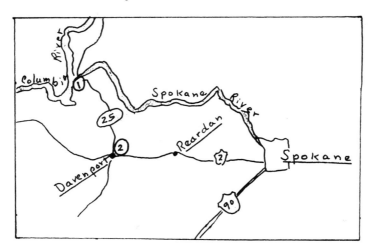

1. Fort Spokane
2. Lincoln County Historical Museum

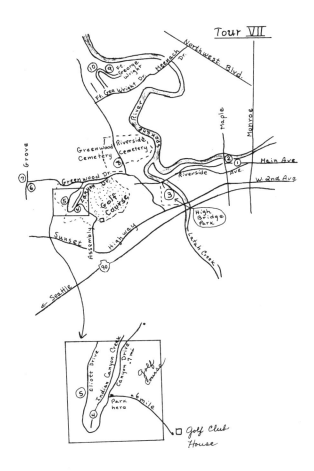

1. Glover Field
2. Peaceful Valley
3. High Bridge Park
4. Indian Canyon Falls
5. Last Homesite of Spokan Garry
6. Little Red Schoolhouse
7. Greenwood House
8. Spokan Garry's Grave
9. Ft. George Wright
10. St. Michael's Mission Church

# TOUR VII

## 1. GLOVER FIELD

Named for James N. Glover, founder of Spokane, this field can be found at the foo of West Main Street. It has had many varied uses, such as: a favorite picnic ground in earl years; traveling shows and circuses performed here; so did dog, horse, and chicken show Later track and baseball events were held. At one time the Sportsman Shows took place a Glover field.

On the north side of Main Street above the field is a large block of granite intended t be the base for a life-size statue of Jim Glover. Although the base was installed for th formal dedication of Glover Field in 1917, the rest of the project, obviously, was neve finished.

## 2. PEACEFUL VALLEY

Former names for the area west of the Monroe Street Bridge and below Riversid Avenue were Spring Flat and Poverty Flat. When Charles Clough platted it in 1891, h gave it the name of Peaceful Valley. Franz Pietsch, a brick mason and gardener, built th first brick house in the valley in 1891. It still stands on the S.E. corner of Main and Ontari (Ash) Streets. By 1900 a large number of Finlanders and some German and Italia immigrants lived there.

This was a traditional salmon fishing and campground for the Middle Spokan: Fourth and Pine in Browne's Addition, Garden Springs, Cowley Park and Drumhelle Springs were used as winter campgrounds by the Indians.

## 3. HIGH BRIDGE PARK

Situated along Hangman Creek, the old Union Pacific Railroad trestle which gav this park its name was removed in January, 1979. This was also a former Indian campin site.

## 4. INDIAN CANYON FALLS

Just west of Indian Canyon Golf Course is a miniature canyon carrying Canyo Creek. At the head of it is a lovely little falls.

(See map inset. From Government Way turn west onto Greenwood Drive for .3 of a mile. Go south on Canyon Driv for .7 of a mile. Here the road turns left, but park on the dirt road. A small sign on a tree says: Indian Canyon Parl About 60 ft. On the right is the canyon and falls.

## 5. LAST HOMESITE OF SPOKAN GARRY

(About ¼ of a mile from the falls along the dirt road (Elliot Drive) one will find the wooden marker.)

Spokan Garry was given permission by Mr. Mouet, owner of the property, to pitch h tepee on this flat after being driven away from the banks of Hangman Creek in Peacefu Valley. With his blind wife, Nina, he stayed here until his death in 1892. Garry ha become a dispirited and disillusioned man—caught between the advance of the whit population and the unchanging ways of the Redman.

(Elliot Drive is badly rutted, and unless one has a four-wheel drive vehicle, it is not recommended to drive in

## 6. LITTLE RED SCHOOLHOUSE *

Do you remember the Little Red Schoolhouse? Here 'tis! Constructed in 1902 th wood frame building is the last example of the one-room school in the Spokane area

Occident School was built during the time when the rural school children of all grades were taught together in the same room.

(It is at the intersection of Grove and Greenwood Roads.)

## 7. GREENWOOD HOUSE

A fellow named Greenwood built the long building kitty-corner across the road from the Occident School in 1909 as a combination house, horse barn, and chicken house. He sold to Getches, who used it for his horses and as a harness shop for his livery stable on West Second Avenue.

## 8. SPOKAN GARRY'S GRAVE

Spokan Garry and his wife were buried at Greenwood Cemetery near the entrance. A beautiful granite monument was placed at the grave site by the Spokane Garry Chapter of the Daughters of the American Revolution, 1925. It truly can be said that *"Garry was born, died, and was buried within a few miles of the land he loved so much."*

## 9. FORT GEORGE WRIGHT †, 1889-1958.

This military post was named for Col. George Wright, who led the retributions against the Indians following Col. Steptoe's defeat in 1858. (See Tours IV and V.) Until recently the Fort Wright College Campus occupied 76 acres of the original army base. About 19 of the buildings date from the early days of the post, 1899-1906.

(Fort Wright can be approached either from Government Way or Northwest Blvd. *via* the Meenach Drive bridge.)

## 10. ST. MICHAEL'S MISSION CHURCH *, 1908.

At the end of the road beyond the Commons stands a little brown church. In 1968 it was moved from Palmer Road for preservation and restoration. The timbers framing the structure were cut with a broad axe and shaped with an adze. The square nails were made by hand, as was all the decorative trim. Except for the organ and stove, all the furnishings and artifacts are original. This was the third mission building which served as school, meeting place and church for the Indians. (See Tour III, Nos. 2 and 3.)

St. Michael's Mission Church

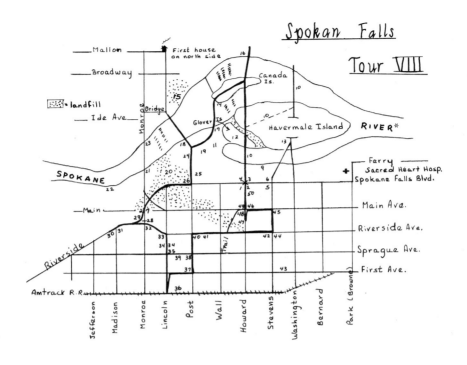

Spokan Falls

Tour VIII

X FOUR CORNERS * Start here.

| | | | |
|---|---|---|---|
| 1. | James N. Glover's Store, 1876 | 26. | City Hall Historical Plaque |
| 2. | Glover's First Separate Dwelling | 27. | Main Street Fill |
| 3. | California House | 28. | Ensign Monaghan Statue |
| 4. | Glover & Gilliam Livery Stable | 29. | Spokane Club |
| 5. | Masterson's Boarding House | 30. | Our Lady of Lourdes Cathedral |
| 6. | Hunsaker's Grocery Store | 31. | 1923 — "Best money can buy." |
| 7. | Early Jail | 32. | The Review Tower |
| 8. | Army Officers' Quarters | 33. | Empire State Building |
| 9. | Carousel | 34. | Dead-end Alleys |
| 10. | First Bridge, 1881 | 35. | Germond Block |
| 11. | Scranton & Downing's Sawmill | 36. | Fire of 1889 started here |
| 12. | Echo Roller Mill | 37. | Pennington Hotel |
| 13. | Gt. Northern Clock Tower, 1902 | 38. | Davenport's Restaurant |
| 14. | Water Pumping Plant, 1888 | 39. | Davenport Hotel |
| 15. | Land Fill & 2nd Hydroelectric Plant | 40. | Great Eastern Building |
| 16. | The Flour Mill | 41. | Kuhn Building |
| 17. | Historical Marker, Suspension Bridge | 42. | Fernwell Building |
| 18. | C & C Flour Mill | 43. | Fire Station No. 1 |
| 19. | Bassett Cabin | 44. | Glover's Residence, 1881 |
| 20. | Land Fill | 45. | 1889 Building, Bodie Block |
| 21. | Monroe St. Power Plant, 1889 | 46. | Bennett Block |
| 22. | Glover Field & Peaceful Valley | 47. | Duffy & Butler's Saloon, 1897 |
| 23. | Piers from 1892 Monroe St. Bridge | 48. | Frankfurt Block |
| 24. | Washington Water Power Sign | 49. | Graham's Hall, County Offices, 1881 |
| 25. | Gondola | 50. | Coeur d'Alene Hotel |

# TOUR VIII

## SPOKAN FALLS ‡ — A DOWNTOWN WALKING TOUR.

‡ (The controversy over the spelling of Spokane can be considered to have been settled November 29, 1881 when Spokane Falls was officially incorporated with the final *e*. In 1890 the "Falls" was dropped.)

1. On the southwest corner of Howard and Front Streets **Jim Glover** built a two-story, frame building in 1876. It housed a number of "firsts": the post office, bank, city hall, theatre and public meeting hall. Besides the enlarged store, this was the community's social center with dances held upstairs.

2. Jasper Matheny, Glover's partner, lived on the southeast corner of Howard and Front until 1876 when he decided there was no future in the town by the falls and asked Glover to buy him out. Upon his departure the Glovers moved to this site and enlarged the log cabin into a five-room house with a picket fence. In so doing, they created **GLOVER'S FIRST SEPARATE DWELLING.**

✗ **FOUR CORNERS.** * This intersection of Howard Street and Spokane Falls Blvd. can be said to have been the hub of the tiny village of Spokan Falls. Called Front Street at first, the name was changed around 1913 to Trent Avenue. In 1973 it was changed again to Spokane Falls Boulevard before the opening of Expo '74.

The Story of Spokane really began in 1871 when a couple of characters by the names of Seth Scranton and John Downing came over the Mullan Road from Montana. It is said they were on the run from a U.S. Marshal for horse stealing and cattle rustling. Whatever . . . they liked the campsite by the falls, stayed, and built a small sawmill.

Now it happened that on May 11, 1873, **JAMES N. GLOVER** from Salem, Oregon, arrived upon the scene. Accompanied by Jasper Matheny, Glover was scouting the upper country for a location likely to be on the route of a transcontinental railroad, the Northern Pacific. The Falls could easily fit the description. Since Scranton and Downing were eager to sell, Glover bought them out for $4000. Included was their squatter's claim of 160 acres. The acreage made an inverted "T" covering the area from Bernard Street west to Cedar Street and Sprague Avenue north to the river. The stem of the "T" was 40 acres taking in the lower falls and extending across the river to Broadway Avenue.

In November, 1873 Glover opened his **FIRST STORE** on the west side of Howard Street between Front and the river with Indians primarily for his first customers. The Glovers lived next to the store, it being described as two box-houses put together. Because Glover was the first permanent settler, he has been recognized as the "Father of Spokane."

3. **CALIFORNIA HOUSE.** William C. Gray came from California in August, 1878 and bought the northeast corner of this intersection for a hotel. This famous and first hotel faced Front Street. In the back toward the river were the horse corral and pig pens. A favorite story frequently told by Clara Gray happened in January, 1879. They were living in the unfinished hotel, and Mrs. Gray had improvised a closet by hanging a sheet over the wall boards and placing her dresses on pegs. In January the town decided to have a dance at Glover's Hall to raise money for a school house. When Mrs. Gray went to get her black silk dress for the party, she found the lace frozen to the wall boards! A heated flat iron did the trick, as she literally ironed it off the wall. she made it to the dance and waltzed the first waltz in town.

May 17, 1877, California House suffered a severe fire. Rebuilt and enlarged, it was renamed The Windsor, still the town's leading hotel. However, the big fire of 1889 demolished this pioneer hostelry for all time.

**4.** On the fourth corner (NW) stood the **GLOVER & GILLIAM LIVERY STABLES.** John, a younger brother of Jim Glover's, with Lane Gilliam—who became the town's first town marshal—were the proprietors.

**5.** Down the street (SW corner of Stevens Street and Spokane Falls Blvd.) stood **MASTERSON'S BOARDING HOUSE.** With rough accommodations at best, it could only take four or five roomers at a time. Later it became the Western Hotel.

**6.** Directly north (where the Opera House sign is) was another very early **GROCERY STORE—HUNSAKER'S.**

**7.** Oh yes, there was an early **JAIL**, too. It stood on Front Street on the south side between Howard and Mill Streets.

**8.** North across the street was the approximate location of the **ARMY OFFICERS' QUARTERS** during the Nez Perce Indian War of 1877.

**9.** Stop at the **CAROUSEL** † in Riverfront Park. It first offered rides in Natatorium Park (at the west end of Boone Avenue along the Spokane River) in 1909. It took Charles Looff, a German woodcarver, two years to hand carve these beautiful wooden animals. For a number of years the Merry-Go-Round was in storage after the closing of Nat Park in 1963. This is one of the few hand-carved carousels in operation in the United States. Take a ride; you might catch the brass ring. Hours: Approximately May 26 through Labor Day: Daily 11 a.m. to 10 p.m. Call 456-5512 for other operating times.

Lynda Cochran on the Carousel

**10.** On the northwest corner of the Howard Street Bridge is a **MARKER** commemorating the place, 100 feet north of the Great Northern Depot, where the people took refuge and put up log fortifications during the Nez Perce scare of August, 1877.

**THE FIRST BRIDGE** in town crossed the river at this location in 1881. It ran from here diagonally across the island and spanned the north channel about Washington Street. Notice on the map that Glover's Island was once separate, but the channel was filled in partly with rubble from the Spokane fire, making one large island. Later, Washington Water Power dammed the south river channel to provide power for a sawmill, thus creating the forebay or lagoon in Riverfront Park.

**1.** Downstream was **SCRANTON AND DOWNING'S SAWMILL** built in 1871, the first structure at Spokan Falls. It was described as being at the foot of Mill (Wall) Street and a little to the west. Jim Glover arrived here May 11, 1873 and bought into partnership. The mill stood bout one-half block south of the present Washington Water Power generating plant. For 73 years a sawmill operated at this location. The riverbank today is not the same as it was one hundred years ago. Some of the smaller channels have been filled in and the large rock outcroppings have been dynamited out.

**2.** The second flour mill at Spokan Falls was the **ECHO ROLLER MILL** built in 1882 by the Rev. Samuel G. Havermale and George A. Davis on Glover's Island.

**3. GREAT NORTHERN CLOCK TOWER \***, all that is left of the Great Northern Railroad Depot, 1902-1972, serves as a monument to the contributions made by railroading to the development of the Inland Empire.

**4.** From the next section of the Howard Street Bridge, along the southern edge of Cannon (or Canada) Island and just at the northern end of the Suspension Foot Bridge some brickwork can be seen. They are all that remain of the **WATER PUMPING PLANT**

**Brick Remnants of the Water Pumping Plant**

built in 1888 to provide drinking water for the town. These sections of brick walls are the only remnants left of our earliest industrial buildings. At low water part of the concrete foundation can be seen in the riverbed, especially from the Suspension Bridge. This early water works was abandoned about 1896 because of sewage (pollution) in the river. The building was torn down in 1923.

15. Directly west is the Black Angus Restaurant. Prior to 1940 there was an eddy of the river at that location. In 1886 Spokane's second **HYDROELECTRIC PLANT** was erected there by the Spokane Falls Electric Light and Power Co. A year earlier George Fitch had installed a small generator in the Echo Flour Mill which produced enough kilowatts to illuminate 10 arc lights. Spokane was the first city west of the Mississippi River to use water power to generate electricity. This was only three years after Thomas Edison built a steam plant in New Jersey. The eddy was filled-in about 1940.

16. On the north side of the river stands **THE FLOUR MILL †**, West 621 Mallon. Built about 1895 the Flour Mill was sold to Portland Mills who operated it until July, 1972. The next year the building was remodeled into interesting shops and restaurants.

When visiting The Mill, look for the remains of the circular grain bins on the east side of the building. The Mill was operated by a system of belts powered by water until the mid-1930s when an electric motor was installed. The wheels used as a railing on the east side were part of that belt power system. The front of the building and the west storehouse were added during the 1930s or 1940s. As you go down the ramp toward Klinkerdagger's, notice the walls made of 2x4s. These were the walls for the grain bins. As the grain came down into the bins, it wore away the wood, leaving these unusual groove-like markings. (One enters the building on the 4th level. This grooving is particularly noticeable on the 3rd and 2nd levels also.) The original floor is still in use on the 3rd level. The flour was stored in the brick part of the building on the west. One can also see how the river has been altered by filling in between the large rock outcroppings which at one time were islands.

Return by way of Canada Island to the Suspension Bridge. Here one can get a closer look at the brick work from the Water Pumping Plant.

17. Don't miss the **HISTORICAL MARKER** at the south end of the Suspension Bridge. It tells about Spokane's Great Fire. Although the little water pumping plant has been accused of failing the city in its hour of need, the problem lay with the crew who had been working on the water main at the foot of Post Street that day. The shut-off valve on the pipe had not been re-opened. George A. Bartoo, chief engineer, had plenty of pressure at the pumping station. After someone went to check the valve on the Post Street main, water got up to the fire. Unfortunately, it was too late. It seems a catastrophe must have a victim, so the "fall guys" were Rolla A. Jones, water superintendent and Bartoo who both lost their jobs.

Cross the YMCA parking lot to the Post Street Bridge. This is the original site of the first Post Street Bridge, 1883. The plaque on the northeast corner of the bridge tells its history. The old wooden toll bridge was such a rickety structure that it had to be weighted down with sandbags during high water so it wouldn't collapse into the river.

## 18. CLARK & CURTIS FLOUR MILL

Where the Washington Water Power Substation stands (1910) stood the Clark & Curtis Flour Mill, 1885, the third mill in Spokane Falls. Built to the north of Frederick Post's 1876 mill, the mill shows up prominently as the C & C in many early-day photographs. It was possibly the first flour mill in the area to ship flour to the eastern part of the country.

Courtesy Eastern Washington State Historical Society

**19.** Near the sawmill in a **CABIN** shared with bachelor Scranton, lived the Wilbur Fiske **BASSETTS**. Bassett was employed by Scranton & Downing to help build their sawmill. January 2, 1872 Minnie Maria Bassett was born, the first all-white child born at Spokan Falls. Later that year the family moved to the Granite Lake area where Minnie Maria drowned at the age of 1½ years. Her grave can still be seen on a hillside. (See Tour IV, No. 5.)

**20.** Take a good look at the south shore between the rock outcroppings. This is all **LAND FILL.** There was a gulch over 100 feet deep that ran from here in a southeastward direction coming out level about Howard and Riverside. The stream in this gully came from the spring in Cowley Park (7th and Division Street).

Because development along the river front was restricted by this deep ravine, Spokan Falls grew south, making Howard Street the principal street in town. From the very beginning the early citizens started filling in this giant hole. The City Hall, the Woolworth Building, Skaggs, part of Nordstrom's, and the Crescent Department Store are all or partially on filled land.

**21.** The **MONROE STREET STATION** came "on the line" November 12, 1890 closing down the Central Station in the bay of the river. Built by Washington Water Power near the south end of the Monroe Street Bridge, this power plant is probably the oldest hydroelectric plant in the country still in commission.

**22.** Further west beyond the Monroe Street Bridge is **GLOVER FIELD** in **PEACEFUL VALLEY** where once large grandstands stood against the bank for the spectators at sporting events.

**23.** Three bridges have spanned the river at Monroe Street. The first, a sway-backed, wooden affair, lasted only nine months, burning July 23, 1890. The **MASONRY PIERS** on which the 1892 steel structure stood can still be seen under the north end of the Monroe Street Bridge. When the present bridge opened for traffic November 23, 1911, it was considered the longest concrete arch bridge in the United States.

41

**24.** Returning south on Post Street stop to read the **SIGN** by the **WASHINGTON WATER POWER SUBSTATION**. Note the unusual green color in some of the bricks on this building designed by Kirtland Cutter.

**25.** The little blue **GONDOLA** cars operated during Expo '74 traveling "over the falls and under the bridge." If they are running, treat yourself to a neat ride, or call 456-5512 for hours of operation.

**26.** On the Post and Spokane Falls Blvd. corner of **CITY HALL** is a **HISTORICAL PLAQUE** noting the former occupants of this site. The first resident was Frederick Post who built a two-story house here in 1876. To the west of City Hall on Spokane Falls Blvd. is a relief map sign depicting various locations in pioneer Spokan Falls.

**27.** At the intersection of Main Avenue and Monroe Street you are standing on landfill. Originally Main Avenue went *under* the Monroe Street Bridge. During the 1910 era a project was started to fill in and bring Main up to the level of Riverside. The dirt came from the excavations of the city-wide sewer system. This project was finished abut 1924. The site of the Public Library, W. 906 Main Avenue, was filled about 1900. The Spokane Club Recreational Building, Main and Monroe, is also on filled land; in fact, it was once the location of the city's public trash dump.

The cave-in of the southern approach to the Monroe Street Bridge in the summer of 1979 recalled the old wooden bridge over Main Avenue that connected Monroe Street with the bridge. What a sharp reminder that our past is not all that long ago.

**28. ENSIGN MONAGHAN STATUE** stands at the intersection of Riverside Avenue and Monroe Street in front of the Spokane Club. John Robert Monaghan was born in Chewelah, WA, March 26, 1873. When Gonzaga College (high school) opened in 1887, he became one of the first twenty students. Upon graduation at the age of 18, he took the entrance examinations for both West Point and Annapolis, scoring the highest grades in the country at both schools. Choosing the Naval Academy, Monaghan served in the South Pacific after graduating in 1895. During a jungle skirmish with the natives on Samoa at the time of the Spanish-American War, a superior officer was wounded. Ensign Monaghan refused to leave him, giving his life in the line of duty.

A hero's burial was given the young officer's body when it was returned to Spokane. On October 26, 1906 the Monaghan family presented this bronze statue to the citizens of the State of Washington. In further recognition of Ensign Monaghan's service to his country, a torpedo boat destroyer was named for him.

**29.** The **SPOKANE CLUB**, W. 1002 Riverside Avenue, was designed by Spokane's famed architect, Kirtland K. Cutter and built in 1910. The fireplace in the library is the second largest in the state. Next door is the **CHAMBER OF COMMERCE** building, W. 1020 Riverside. Note the Indian heads at the top of the columns of this 1931 building. To the west at W. 1108 Riverside is the **MASONIC TEMPLE**, 1905.

**30. OUR LADY OF LOURDES**, W. 1115 Riverside Avenue, the Cathedral of the Spokane Catholic Diocese, was begun in 1902 and completed about 1908. A school (now closed) and rectory were added later.

**31.** The "best money can buy" in 1923 is the way this building was advertised when built for the Great Northwest Life Insurance Company at W. 1023 Riverside Ave. It has been the **CHANCERY** for the **CATHOLIC** Diocese since 1965.

**32. THE REVIEW TOWER** †, Monroe and Riverside. This building has become a landmark in Spokane because of the unusual shape. Built after the fire and dedicated October 24, 1891, it enjoyed the reputation of being the tallest building in town for ten years. The sixth floor comprised a penthouse apartment to which W.H. Cowles, publisher, brought his bride in 1896. His office was on the seventh floor until after World War I.

Cowles made many contributions to the community, among which are Camp Cowles, the Boy Scout Camp on Diamond Lake, which was developed on land donated by Cowles; and the Cheney Cowles Museum, a memorial to his son killed in World War II.

(Do take time to enter the lobby through the revolving doors. Note the marble walls, the ornate and beautifully carved wood trim and the grill work.)

The first Presbyterian Church in Spokane (organized 1883) worshipped in a small frame structure on this corner in 1886. Later the same building was used to house a pioneer newspaper, *The Spokane Falls Review.*

Directly east the Cowles Publishing Company erected a new headquarters for the *Spokesman Review* and *Chronicle* newspapers, but retained the curved front. The preceeding **CRESCENT BUILDING** was one of the few buildings to escape the fire of 1889. At that time a brand-new merchandising firm occupied space on the ground floor, taking its name from the shape of the building. Later it moved to its present location, but retained the old name, the Crescent. On the first floor of the department store by the clock is a piece of granite bearing the Crescent name. This came from the top of the old Crescent Building.

**33. EMPIRE STATE BUILDING,** W. 907 Riverside Ave., currently referred to as the Great Western Building, was billed as the first fire-proof building in town. Construction started in 1898. It had electric elevators housed in an open steel cage-like shaft in the center of the building. Very modern, indeed! (The center of the building above the first floor is still open, and the cages for those elevators can be seen although enclosed ones have since been installed.) At the time of the fire in 1889, the Commercial Hotel was on this corner. In order to save it and confine the fire, buildings were dynamited along Lincoln Street which included the police station.

**34.** South on Lincoln about half-way between Riverside and Sprague are **DEAD-END ALLEYS** on both sides of the street. After the fire the city planners replotted the business district with the idea of providing an alleyway approach east-to-west through each block. The property owners were asked to donate 8 feet at the back of their properties to the city for alleys. Between Spokane Falls Blvd. and Main Ave., and between Main and Riverside the alleys were built from Division to Lincoln. But, south of Riverside this didn't always work out. Apparently, some easements were never recorded at the Court House. Consequently, Spokane has ended up with some alleys that go nowhere, as you can see.

In other incidents the property was purchased as tax delinquent and narrow 16-foot alleyway buildings were erected. The Sartori Building on Wall Street was the last one left; now it, too, has disappeared.

**35. GERMOND BLOCK** on the northeast corner of Sprague and Lincoln is one of Spokane's oldest commercial buildings, having been built in 1890. There were two major entrances through the cut-off southwest and northwest corners. The one on the alley led to the Log Cabin Saloon. Further down the alley is a large arch through which the brewery wagons rolled in the barrels. Eugene Germond was a pioneer saloon keeper, having settled in Spokane prior to 1884.

One other major tenant in the building was the city whose offices were located here until the new City Hall (now the old, old) was built on the California House site in 1892.

**36.** Two blocks further south is a wider than usual alley which is about the location of Railroad Avenue, the street just north of the railroad tracks. Until the railroad tracks were elevated in 1914, there were ten sets of tracks to go across whenever one journeyed to or from the south part of town. On the north side of Railroad Avenue, the fourth building east from Lincoln Street, was Wolfe's Lunch Counter with a lodging house on the second floor. It was here, most authorities agree, **THE FIRE STARTED** about 6:15 p.m. on a hot Sunday, August 4, 1889. One version is that a roomer by the name of Irish Kate was in her room getting ready for the evening trade at the saloon where she was a "hostess." As was the practice of the time, she put her curling iron in the chimney of an oil lamp to heat. She had an unexpected masculine caller; an argument arose. The subsequent scuffle knocked over the table and lamp, setting the curtains on fire. Shortly, Spokane Falls was ablaze. (Actually, there are at least four versions as to how the fire got started; no one knows. This one just happens to make a good story.)

Within ten minutes the fire department arrived upon the scene. They connected hoses at hydrant after hydrant, but there was no water pressure. Creating its own wind, the fire swept its way through the tinder-dry buildings toward the river. In order to contain the fire, the buildings along Lincoln and Washington Streets were dynamited. Within four hours the fire reached the river, and 32 buildings within 27 city blocks were no more.

**37.** Return to First Avenue, then one block east to Post Street. The **PENNINGTON HOTEL** on the northwest corner began as the Bellevue House in 1893, then became The Pennington. As noted below, it came under Louie Davenport's ownership ten years later. This part of the Davenport Hotel is no longer used.

**38.** On the north half of the block stands the 1890 Wilson Block. For nearly one hundred years **DAVENPORT'S RESTAURANT** has been located here. Louis Davenport came to town in the spring of 1889. Among other odd jobs he worked for the "Pride of Spokane" Restaurant as a buyer and general utility man. Just two days before The Fire he bought the restaurant which was located on the east side of Howard near Sprague Avenue (the north part of the present Merton Block).

More pick-and-shovel work followed the fire before he opened a "waffle foundry" in a tent just north of the Davenport Hotel on West Sprague. (For a year-and-a-half or so after the fire until reconstruction was completed, Spokane businesses operated in various sized tents.) July 4, 1890 Davenport moved his restaurant into the Wilson Block. By 1903 he owned both the Wilson and Pennington, unifying them with a Spanish Mission-style exterior.

**39. DAVENPORT HOTEL** †, 1914, W. 807 Sprague Ave. Louie Davenport became nationally famous as a restauranteer and hotel man. Over the years many celebrities have stayed here. Designed by Kirtland K. Cutter, its ornate trim, beautiful, spacious ballrooms, and uncrowded lobby belong to a past era — "Spokane's Age of Elegance."

It is said that during Prohibition Mr. Davenport's former apartment over the restaurant was used for private parties. The elaborate, key-shaped design on the doors served as one-way peep holes to watch for law enforcement agents. In case of a raid, the guests could exit unnoticed through connecting rooms.

For many years the Davenport Hotel carried on the tradition of never letting the fire burn out in the large lobby fireplace, summer or winter. Another lost custom was washing all the coins received every night. How they shone!

Group tours of the hotel can be arranged through their Sales Office: Monday-Friday, 9 a.m.-4 p.m. No charge.

**40.** One block north on the southwest corner of Post and Riverside is the Peyton Building, N. 10 Post. Constructed in 1890 as the **GREAT EASTERN**, it suffered a disastrous fire January 24, 1898. It began in the basement of John W. Graham's and claimed nine lives. Col. I.N. Peyton purchased the burned-out shell and rebuilt the five stories, changing the name to The Peyton. In 1902 he incorporated the three-story Hogan Block directly south, adding two stories to match the Peyton. Seven years later Col. Peyton completed the building by erecting a 7-story annex south to Sprague and adding two more levels to his older buildings.

**41.** (For a better view, walk along the north side of Riverside Avenue.) Midway between Post and Wall on the south side of Riverside stand twin buildings: the Van Valkenburg and the Holland Blocks, erected in 1890. In 1902 Aaron Kuhn, a banker from Colfax, bought the buildings, remodeled them into one, and placed his own name on the front. The upper floors of the **KUHN BUILDING** have been vacant for many years. Hopefully, the building will be restored and preserved, thus remaining as a direct link to our past.

**42.** One of the few remaining 1890 buildings on Riverside Avenue is the **FERNWELL** at Riverside and Stevens. Designed by Herman Preusse and built by Rollin H. Hyde, it was originally known as the Chamber of Commerce Building. In 1893 the name became the Fernwell.

**43. FIRE STATION NO. 1,** W. 418 First Avenue. On the north side of First Ave. between Stevens and Washington Streets is a small brick building painted gray. Above the entrance can still be seen: "Station No. 1 — S.F.D." Built in 1890, a three-horse-drawn hook and ladder wagon plus the men who handled them were housed here. The horses, stabled in the basement, were trained to get into position in front of the hose wagon when the fire alarm sounded. It took only five snaps to connect the harness which dropped from above. Within 30 seconds the equipment hit the street. After replacing the horses by motorized trucks in 1911, the last fire truck drove out in 1933. The holes for the fire poles are still visible in the metal ceiling.

**44.** The southeast corner of Stevens Street and Riverside Avenue where the Paulsen Medical Building stands is where Jim and Susan Glover built a home in 1881. After the block was sold to F.M. Tull for $10,000 in 1877, the house was moved to 1725 West First Avenue in Browne's Addition where it can still be seen. (See Tour IX, No. 1.)

**45. 1889 BUILDING**, the Brodie Block, a small building on the southeast corner of Main Avenue and Stevens Street was restored in 1973-1974. Immediately south is the **LEVY BLOCK** constructed in 1892.

**46.** As you walk along the north side of Main Avenue between Stevens and Howard Streets look at the **CURBS. GRANITE** cut in 10-foot segments was used in the downtown area for curbing during the reconstruction era after the Fire of 1889. **HITCHING RINGS** can also be seen in this block: rings set into the curb to tie up one's horse and/or buggy.

Granite curbs can also be found along Washington, Stevens, Howard Streets, the south side of Riverside Aveune, South Monroe, as far north as Broadway Ave., and as far south as Second Avenue.

On the northeast corner at W. 530 Main Avenue, is the 1889 **BENNETT BLOCK**. It was built by A.M. Cannon's son-in-law. The attractive restoration in 1978 included five buildings. In the early 1900s the Hotel Savoy occupied the upper stories.

**47.** N. 117 Howard. This small brick building built around 1891 was **DUFFY AND BUTLER'S SALOON** in 1897. The old metal ceiling is still in use, and sections of the original brick walls have been exposed.

Half a block north, on the northeast corner was the Grand Hotel (The Bon Marche is on the site.) Spokane was a tough town even in the late nineties. In the summer of 1897 a well-known New York writer, Hamlin Garland, came to town to get some Western color for the stories he was writing. When asked where to look for some real "Wild West" action, Marshal Joel Warren told him just to watch the street in front of his hotel.

**Duffy and Butler's Saloon, 1897**

As the story goes, that Saturday night a Texan came out of Duffy and Butler's Saloon and started shooting up the town. He gunned down two elderly men before the Marshal could get there. A bullet clipped a button off Warren's coat before he could draw his gun. Since the Texan kept firing, the Marshal had to shoot him. As the body was carried away, Garland came out of the Grand Hotel, suitcase in hand. "Did you see that?" Warren asked. "See it? I darn near felt it. Those bullets were bouncing all over the lobby," the writer answered and took the next train back to New York City.

**48.** Just to the north where the Washington Mutual Savings Bank is Holly's Hardware stood on the corner in the 1880s. In 1888 "Dutch" Jake Goetz and his partner Harry Baer began construction on an elaborate, huge, 4-story brick, the **FRANKFURT BLOCK.** Besides providing prestigious office space, it contained Goetz' & Baer's lavish saloon. The gala opening took place in the middle of July, 1889. Two weeks later there were only smoldering ruins.

**49.** Tremendous rivalry existed between Spokan Falls and Cheney for the county seat. Cheney won the election, but the Falls had the records. Shortly after midnight March 21, 1881 about a dozen Cheneyites took matters into their own hands. Leaving their horses on Riverside, they crept along the trail across the gulch to **GRAHAM'S HALL** on the northwest corner of Main and Howard. They rescued the county records from the second floor offices and returned home. "Stole them!" accused the Spokanites the next morning. But, in Cheney they remained until an election in 1886 returned the county seat to Spokane permanently.

**50. COEUR D'ALENE HOTEL,** N. 232 Howard Street, is owned by the Milner Corporation. This is the site where Glover's partner Matheny lived in 1873, then the Glovers. After they moved, F.R. Moore and August Goldsmith established a general merchandise store on this corner. Subsequent owners were Charles Sweeny and the Loewenberg Brothers: Bernard and Herman. After the Fire of 1889, the Loewenbergs replaced the building, but sold in 1894 to "Dutch" Jake and Harry Baer who converted it into the fanciest saloon and gambling casino in town.

**1890 Street Scene**

47

Goetz and Baer had helped grub-stake Noah Kellogg, whose jackass kicked a rock—so the story goes—and discovered the richest silver mine in the Coeur d'Alene Mountains, the Bunker Hill and Sullivan. Their share of its sale was two hundred thousand dollars in 1887. Besides the casino, the Coeur d'Alene contained a variety theatre, turkish bath parlor, dance hall, and a section in the basement where a man could get a bed for the night and one free meal if he were "down on his luck." After gambling became illegal in the State of Washington in 1908, the Coeur d'Alene was converted into a hotel.

Across the street to the north, California House is gone, and in its place rose the first City Hall in 1892. After burning in 1909, it was torn down a year later for the overhead Union Pacific and Milwaukee Railroad tracks and station which were removed for Expo '74.

To the west John Glover had moved his stables to the northeast corner of Front and Bernard, thus escaping the fire. A new building arose on his old site for Maxwell photographers. In 1893 it was another Windsor Hotel which came down in 1913 for the overhead railroad trackage.

Back to Glover's store location. Jim replaced his 1883 building, the second brick in town, with the Pioneer Block after the fire. It was demolished in 1977.

Before leaving, take a look south down Howard Street. The east side is surely a scene straight from the early 1890s.

California House

# TOUR IX

## SPOKANE'S "AGE OF ELEGANCE"

During the 1880s and 1890s tremendous wealth poured into Spokane from the mining regions of the Coeur d'Alenes and British Columbia and from railroading. Fortunes were also made in real estate and from the developing city. The wealthy spent their fortunes by building lavish mansions complete with matching carriage houses and luxurious interiors. They owned fine horses, wore grand clothes and beautiful jewelry, and hired the servants to care for it all. Fortunately, there lived in Spokane a superb young architect by the name of Kirtland K. Cutter. Many of the following mansions were designed by him. There were several fashionable residential areas as Spokane had no "right or wrong" side of the tracks. However, Browne's Addition and "The Hill" were pretty much the most distinctive.

In sharp contrast to this lovely and social period was the world outside the mansions. The downtown streets were just being paved in 1898; there was mud or dust depending on the season, and the horse "droppings" knew no season. Street lights ran no further west than Maple Street. Spokane was wide open with gambling emporiums and their "painted ladies," and numerous variety theatres. (For a graphic picture of the era, read Margaret Bean's *Age of Elegance* available at Cheney Cowles Museum.)

(To reach Browne's Addition take West Riverside jogging onto West First past the Maple Street Bridge, or follow West Second Avenue.)

49

# 1. "THE GLOVER," 1881, West 1725 First Avenue.

James N. Glover built this home on the southeast corner of Stevens and Riverside Avenue. It was made of hand-hewn timbers and hand-wrought nails. After being moved to this site, it was purchased by Wm. Pettet for his daughter and son-in-law, the J.P.M. Richards in 1887. (Richards, with his brother Henry and R.L. Rutter, founded the Spokane and Eastern Trust Bank.) A son of Richards lived in the house until 1959. The house was extensively remodeled in 1911 and during World War II. It is now apartments.

The stained glass windows between the chimney flues on the west side of the house are most unusual although they were not part of the original structure.

"The Glover," 1881, West 1725 First Avenue

# 2. RUTTER HOUSE, 1895, West 1727 Pacific Avenue, an Arts and Crafts cottage.

Robert Lewis Rutter was president of a life insurance company, vice president and a founder of the Spokane and Eastern Trust Company, director of a railroad and of a title company. He is better known today for the Parkway near the Little Spokane River which bears his name.

# 3. DWIGHT HOUSE, 1887, West 1905 Pacific Avenue.

This Queen Anne styled house was built by Daniel H. Dwight for his bride, Mary P Willis whose family had come to Spokane the year before. The Willis home was next door Dwight became successful in real estate and was a director of the Fidelity National Ban (now First Interstate Bank). He donated the site of their summer home, Brookside," fo the Finch Arboretum. At the time Dwight built his home, Pacific Avenue was only roug graded to Cannon Street. Beyond that was a wagon track winding around the tree stump which had not yet been removed.

In 1927 Dwight gave the tower chimes to Westminster Congregational Church i memory of his wife who had an outstanding singing voice and was a graduate of th Boston Conservatory of Music. Forty-six years later Dwight's daughter, Dorothy F Woodward, presented a stained glass window to the Plymouth Congregational Church South Walnut and 8th Ave. in memory of the Daniel H. Dwight family.

**4. BERNARD LOEWENBERG,** 1890, West 1923 First Avenue.

W.J. Carpenter designed this house for one of the Loewenberg brothers, early merchants whose store was on the southeast corner of Howard Street and Front Avenue (Spokane Falls Boulevard). There is a carriage house. In 1899 Loewnberg and E.J. Roberts (No. 6 below) exchanged houses.

**5. WARREN HUSSEY,** 1893, West 2003 Riverside Avenue.

Viewing this lovely Queen Anne home is like taking a step back to Victorian times. There is beautiful stained glass in the windows especially the vinegar cruet and fruit motif in the dining room. Note also the detailed bay windows and the carriage house to the west which had never been remodeled into something else.

**6. EDWARD J. ROBERTS,** pre-1886, West 2027 First Avenue.

Roberts, a civil engineer, earned fame for locating and constructing the Canadian Pacific Railroad through the Selkirk Mountains from Winnipeg to Vancouver, B.C., in 1885. In 1888 he came to Spokane as the chief engineer for D.C. Corbin in many railroad building enterprises.

**7. JAY P. GRAVES,** 1900, West 2123 First Avenue.

Graves was active in real estate and also made a fortune in the mines. He donated the land and was instrumental in having Whitworth College moved to Spokane from Tacoma. Architets: Cutter & Malmgren; style: Georgian Revival. Carriage house.

In 1911 **AUBREY L. WHITE**, a business associate of Graves, bought the house. White is best remembered for creating the concept of the city Park Board (1907) and for his participation in expanding the park areas in Spokane.

**8. J.J. BROWNE,** 1887, West 2216 First Avenue. (The site is now the parking area for the museum.)

The Brownes arrived in Spokane in 1878 and with A.M. Cannon bought half of Glover's property. Browne homesteaded the area known as Browne's Addition. He built their second home in 1887 on grounds that included the six blocks from Pacific to Riverside and back of the house to Coeur d'Alene Avenue. Mr. Browne, a lawyer, was also in banking and became the first millionaire in the State of Washington. Browne's Mountain was named for him. He moved his family there at the turn of the century. In 1902 Robert Strahorn, a railroad entrepreneur, purchased the house and had Kirtland Cutter remodel it into 20 rooms, 9 baths, 10 fireplaces, and a bowling alley.

The house on Browne's Mountain burned in 1936, and "Strahorn Pines" had to be razed in 1974 as the result of years of neglect and termites.

**9. CHENEY COWLES MEMORIAL MUSEUM,** West 2316 First Avenue.

The W.H. Cowles family presented the building to the city of Spokane for the use of the Eastern Washington State Historical Society. A *must* place to visit: there are interesting Indian exhibits, pioneer artifacts, and changing displays in the art and history galleries. Downstairs is an excellent research library. Gift and book shop. Look for the "Walking Tour of Historic Browne's Addition." Hours: Tues-Sat: 10 a.m. - 5 p.m.; Sun: 2-5 p.m. (Closed Monday). Donations are appreciated.

**10. CAMPBELL HOUSE** †, 1898, also West 2316 First Avenue. (Enter through the Museum.)

Built by Amasa B. Campbell, a mining man, this house of English half-timbered construction has 19 rooms and 9 fireplaces, each different. The golden reception room is authentic Louis XIV French Rococo. The English Tudor drawing room has heavy oak paneling, beamed ceiling, and recessed Gothic fireplace of the Elizabethan style. The sink in the butler's pantry was made of sterling silver, one of three in Spokane. It was used only to polish the silver. The Campbells employed five full-time servants: a cook, two maids, a coachman, and a gardner whose job in winter was to cut the wood for the furnace — a cord a day.

In 1925 the Campbell's daughter presented the home to the Eastern Washington State Historical Society. Since then some of the original furniture has been located and returned. The silver sink mysteriously disappeared in the early days as a museum. Open daily (except Monday) 10 a.m. - 5 p.m.; Sun: 2-5 p.m. No charge, although donations are appreciated. Tour guides are available and should be used for the greatest enjoyment of the house and furnishings.

**11. REED HOUSE**, 1900, West 2315 First Avenue.

Assumed to have been designed by Cutter, this is an "Arts and Crafts" Cottage. Around 1903 or 1904 Aaron Kuhn, a power in financial circles from Colfax, WA., bought the house. Kuhn was in the Traders National Bank and purchased the Van Valkenburg & Holland Blocks (1890) remodeling them into the Kuhn Building.

**12. WILLIAM J.C. WAKEFIELD**, 1900, West 2328 First Avenue.

A prominent attorney who came to Spokane in May, 1889, from Vermont, Mr. Wakefield was also associated with banking, mining and investments. In 1905 he organized the law firm of Wakefield and [A.W.] Witherspoon. Vacuum cleaners were built on each floor for easier cleaning. Following Wakefield's death in 1931, the house was converted into nine apartments.

**13. JOHN A. FINCH**†, 1900, West 2340 First Avenue.

Finch was a good friend and longtime business associate of A.B. Campbell. Cutter featured a column motif in this 18-room mansion that included leaded glass windows in the entry, mahogony pillars and railings on the staircase and an art gallery.

**14. VACHEL LINDSAY**, W. 2318 Pacific Avenue.

Lindsay, the poet, lived in one of these apartments from 1926-1929. Previously he had lived at the Davenport Hotel for two years. Both his children were born in Spokane.

**15. CHINESE CEMETERY,** West end of Pacific Avenue.

During the 1880s there was a Chinese population of several hundred persons. In the Chinese culture a funeral was a very elaborate ceremony usually conducted at the deceased's place of business as well as at his home. Friends attended only by invitation. All the cabs in town would be hired for the parade to the cemetery which was located at the end of Pacific Avenue on land owned by J.J. Browne. This left the rest of Spokane Falls to walk until the funeral was over. Lead by a squealing-type of music played on flutes, the mourners carried inscribed banners made of crepe paper with holes in them. The purpose was to delay any evil spirits that might be following because the spirits had to pick up and string the banners before they could do any harm to the dead. In this way the deceased could be buried before any harm befell him.

Another belief and practice was that the departed person had to be provided with nourishment on his long voyage into the unknown. The grave was piled with great plates of roast beef, chicken and Chinese delicacies. Lighted josh sticks were placed around the burial site to keep the evil spirits away.

In most cases the bodies were later exhumed and sent to China for interment.

### 16. ALONZO M. MURPHEY, 1883, West 2424 Second Avenue.

Although not properly part of the "Age of Elegance," this house is noteworthy for its age, certainly one of the oldest in Spokane. Note the jerkenhead gables.

### 17. JAMES CLARK, 1900, W. 2308 Third Avenue.

The oldest of the three mining Clark Brothers (James, Patrick and Dennis) James managed their large War Eagle Mine at Rossland, B.C. until his death in 1901. (Dennis lived at W. 2325 First Avenue from 1903-1907.) Patrick Clark donated the altar and altar rail at Our Lady of Lourdes Cathedral, and Mrs. James Clark gave one of the large stained glass windows. In 1920 Mrs. Clark sold her home to the Isabella Association and moved to California.

### 18. PATRICK CLARK, 1898, West 2208 Second Avenue.

Architect Cutter traveled to Europe to collect building materials and furnishings for this mansion built by mining man, "Patsy" Clark. The red sandstone trim was shipped from Italy, the ceiling beams were carved in Belgium, and the rugs were woven in Turkey. There were gold plated wall fixtures, Tiffany chandeliers and stained glass windows, and a most superb Grandfather Clock (still ticking in the entry). The house contained a central hot water heating system and was wired for electricity. The architectural styles represent French, Roman, Moorish, Chinese and Egyptian blended together by an an architectural genius.

In the elaborate carriage house lived five horses: two large ones for the landau, two lighter ones for the Spider phaeton, and a driving horse for the two-wheeled cart. For the six Clark children were kept two shetland ponies, a wicker basket cart, two Newfoundland dogs — and a cow!

### 19. COEUR D'ALENE PARK, 1891, Between West Second and Fourth Avenues, and South Spruce to South Chestnut Streets.

Spokane's **FIRST PARK** was donated to the city by J.J. Browne and A.M. Cannon in 1887.

Original 1890 Carriage House at West 2003 Riverside Avenue.

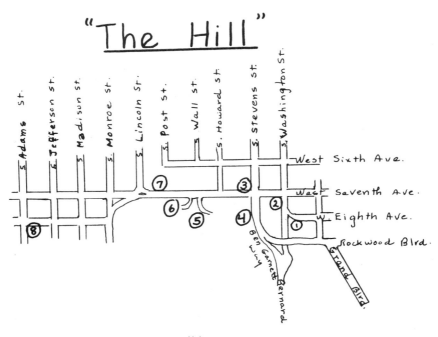

# "THE HILL"

**1. JAMES N. GLOVER,** † 1889, West 321 Eighth Avenue.

This English style baronial home was the first one designed by Kirtland K. Cutter in Spokane. At the time Browne's Addition was "The" residential area, and to build on the hill was considered unusual. The granite came from a quarry on the Little Spokane River, the elaborately carved woodwork was made in Minneapolis, and the furniture manufactured in the east. The twenty-two-room house contained: a gold and white reception room, a two-story entry hall which also had a balcony from the master bedroom suite, and central heating. The most novel feature, however, was the three bathrooms, inside plumbing being virtually unknown at the time. The panic of 1893 nearly bankrupted Glover, forcing him to sell in 1895. (The Patrick Welchs were long-time residents, but since 1942 the Unitarian Church has owned and occupied the property.)

**2. SOUTH 702 WASHINGTON STREET,** 1893.

For thirteen years, 1896-1909, Jimmie Glover lived at this address. During that time he was a receiver for the Northwest Milling and Power Company, served as a city councilman for six years, and was president of the Diamond Ice and Fuel Company.

**3. ROBERT B. PATERSON,** 1904, West 508 Seventh Avenue.

Before building this home in 1904, Paterson of the Spokane Dry Goods Company (The Crescent Department Store) lived at West 417 Seventh Avenue. The Clarence C. Dill family were occupants of this house from 1928-1940 when Senator Dill built a home on the west end of Sumner Avenue overlooking the city. This house is usually referred to as the Dill home.

**4. CORBIN HOUSE,** 1898, West 507 Seventh Avenue.

When built in 1898 on the site of Horace Cutter's (K.K. Cutter's uncle) home, this house sat above the top of Stevens Street. Ben Garnett Way was not cut through until the 1960s. In fact, the carriage house stood right where that street goes today. In 1887 Daniel Chase Corbin built his first railroad from Rathdrum to Coeur d'Alene and from the Old Mission (Cataldo) to Wallace so that the ore from the mines could be transported for processing. From that beginning, D.C. became a railroad tycoon and commissioned his son-in-law, Kirtland K. Cutter, to design this Georgian brick home. Cutter and Mary Corbin had one son, Corbin Cutter, but the marriage ended in divorce. (The Spokane Arts Center occupies the building now.)

**5. F. LEWIS CLARK,** 1896, West 701 Seventh Avenue.

The rear grounds of this English-style home form a park of native wilderness. Like many European homes it is secluded behind a high rock wall. Clark made his first fortune in the C & C (built with Frank E. Curtis) Flour Mill. Then Clark went into mining. In one deal alone he made thirteen million dollars! Known as an "eccentric millionaire," Clark sailed his 105-foot yacht with European royalty. The greatest mystery, never solved, occurred January 17, 1914 when Clark simply vanished in Santa Barbara, California.

In 1909 the Burgess Lee Gordons bought Clark's home, "Undercliff." (Clark had built a large home at Hayden Lake.) The Gordons raised three sons in the 21-room house, adding a ballroom on the third floor in 1919. Mrs. Gordon, after the death of her husband, gave the house and property to the Catholic Bishop of Spokane on August 2, 1929 for a girls' school. Because of her generous gift, the house known as Gordon Hall served as an integral part of the Marycliff High School Campus for 50 years.

## 6. AUSTIN CORBIN, 1898, West 815 Seventh Avenue.

D.C.'s son, Austin, built this southern colonial for $65,000. The grounds for the 17-room mansion covered four acres. The Corbins held a traditional Open House on New Year's Day for the city's elite, which included dancing.

In 1945 Mrs. Corbin donated her home to the Franciscan Sisters, teachers at next door Marycliff High School for girls. The house served as a convent for the Sisters until 1979 when Marycliff closed.

**Austin Corbin Mansion**

## 7. JAMES V. CORBET. West 820 Seventh Avenue.

This Cutter-designed home is still standing.

## 8. BURGESS LEE GORDON, 1895, West 1323 Eighth Avenue.

Gordon was a well-known merchant and wholesale grocer. The granite for the $40,000 house came from the Little Spokane River. Sitting on a slight knoll, the house does look like a "castle," the name of the apartments contained within. (Gordon bought the F. Lewis Clark home on West Seventh Avenue.) Thaddeus S. Lane who was in the telephone and insurance fields and served as a director of 38 companies was the new owner.

At least seven large homes along Seventh Avenue have been removed to make way for apartments and high rise condominiums including Kirtland Cutter's chalet at West 6. There were many other houses along here and further south and southwest, some small some large. Most of the large ones built during the 1890s and early 1900s have been converted into apartments.

# TOUR X

## A CONGLOMERATE OF INTERESTING PLACES

(This grouping encompasses sites, buildings, or events which don't comfortably fit into any other category. They can be observed as one happens to pass by or purposely sought out, whichever.)

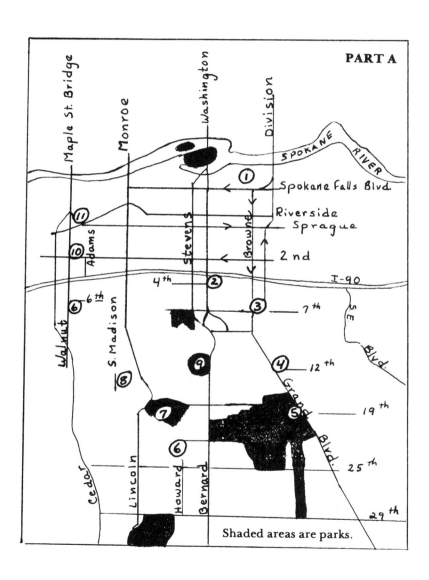

PART A

Maple St. Bridge
Monroe
Washington
Division

SPOKANE RIVER

① Spokane Falls Blvd.

Riverside
Browne
Sprague

Stevens

② 2nd

⑪
Adams

⑩

4th ②

I-90

⑥ 6th

S. Madison

⑨

③ 7th

⑧

④ 12th

Grand Blvd.

Walnut

⑦

⑤ 19th

Cedar
Lincoln
Howard
Bernard

⑥

25th

29th

Shaded areas are parks.

## 1. SACRED HEART HOSPITAL

The Sisters of Providence were invited to build a hospital in Spokane Falls. On April 13, 1886, Mother Joseph, accompanied by Sister Joseph Arimathea who would remain as the first directoress, arrived. They stayed at California House and used the dining room table to draw up plans for their hospital. Work began in June on a 31-room building on Ferry, a block north of Front Avenue about Browne Street. It opened January 15, 1887; the next year a wing was added. The first School of Nursing in the State of Washington began in 1898 at Sacred Heart Hospital. A second wing was added in 1901. When Jim Hill—the well-known railroad magnate—bought the property in 1908, Sacred Heart moved up the hill to 8th and Browne Street.

## 2. WESTMINSTER CONGREGATIONAL CHURCH, † S. 411 Washington Street.

A number of "firsts" can be claimed: the first church in Spokan Falls, organized May 22, 1879, in the Reverend Cowley's home; the oldest standing church building, the cornerstone having been laid September 21, 1890, with completion the next year; and this granite edifice was the first stone building in the Inland Empire.

## 3. COWLEY PARK, † 7th and Division Street.

The Reverend H.T. Cowley, a Presbyterian minister, opened the first public school in 1875. That year the Spokan Falls School District was established. It extended from the Colville River to the Idaho line, and from Spangle to Chewelah. Six children from the town attended the school in Cowley's house as well as the Indian pupils. A monument in the park commemorates Cowley's contributions to early Spokane. Their home was on 6th Avenue between Browne and Division Streets.

## 4. ST. JOHN'S CATHEDRAL, on top of the Grand Boulevard Hill at 12th Avenue

This beautiful church celebrated its Fiftieth Anniversary in 1979. The stained glass windows depict the history of Spokane. Tours by appointment. (The construction of this cathedral lasted from 1926-1954.)

## 5. WATERING TROUGH, 19th and Grand Boulevard.

In 1907 this watering trough was put in for the horses pulling up the long Grand Hill.

## 6. BRICK STREETS

In a number of sections of Spokane the streets were paved with brick. These were made of a particular kind of clay and formed in a special way to be very hard and water repellent which was important in this climate of freezing and thawing cycles. The brick weighed as much as eleven pounds apiece.

Grand Boulevard was bricked in 1909, South Monroe and Lincoln Streets in 1910 and 5th Avenue in 1911. A few of the places where brick streets can still be seen are: South Howard between 21st and 23rd, West 5th Avenue at Jefferson to Adams, 6th Avenue and Cedar, and South Coeur d'Alene Street in Browne's Addition.

## 7. CANNON HILL PARK, 19th and South Lincoln.

In 1886 this site was a brick yard that furnished bricks for some of the early buildings downtown. The business eventually became Washington Brick and Lime.

# 8. STREET CAR TRACKS

On South Madison Street between 14th and 16th Avenues the old street car tracks are still in view.

# 9. CLIFF PARK, 13th and South Grove.

This volcanic rock was once an Indian look-out. A panoramic view of Spokane can be seen from the top of this park donated to the city by the Northern Pacific Railroad.

# 10. WOODEN WAREHOUSE, 1905, South 160 Adams Street.

At one time this was a warehouse for Tull and Gibb's Furniture Store. All that is needed are the horses and buggies for an early century scene.

# 11. JUNCTION OF RIVERSIDE AND SPRAGUE AT CEDAR STREET

The small triangle at this intersection was created when the old frontier Territorial Road from Walla Walla joined the White Bluffs Road from the Columbia River. The White Bluffs Road became Riverside Avenue.

A granite shaft monument was placed in this mini-park by the Spanish-American War Veterans in honor of the only 100% volunteers in the United States Army and Navy n the war with Spain, 1898-1902.

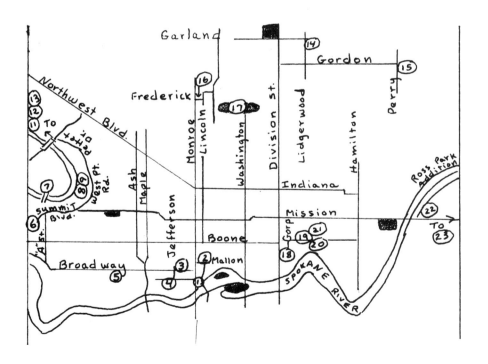

**PART B**

## 1. UNUSUAL WINDOWS, N. 628½ Monroe Street.

Quite fascinating are the windows of this 1905 Holmes Building.* Note the building to the north also.

## 2. FIRST HOUSE ON THE NORTH SIDE, Northeast corner of Mallon and Lincoln.

When Col. David P. Jenkins arrived in Spokane in 1879, no one lived on the north side of the river. No doubt heads were shaking when he took out a homestead from Boone to the river and Post west to Cedar Street. His home was built at what would now be W 820 Mallon. As there were no bridges, he commuted by boat daily to his law office downtown.

When Jenkins donated the land on Broadway and gave $1000 for a courthouse in 1887, the question of its location was settled. In later years his daughter gave the eastern edge of the homestead to the city for the Coliseum.

## 3. SPOKANE COUNTY COURTHOUSE, † W. 1116 Broadway Avenue.

Erected in 1893-1895, the Courthouse was designed by the same architect who designed the State Capitol Building in Olympia, W.A. Ritchie. The architectural style resembles a French chateau. At the time of construction it was portrayed as the finest courthouse in the West and was to be the focal point of a park south to the river. The building cost $340,000, but it proved too costly to complete the park. Washington Brick and Lime of Clayton (at that time) made the bricks. Note the two small hitching rings in the sidewalk approaching the south entrance to the Courthouse.

## 4. SPOKANE METHODIST COLLEGE, College Avenue and Jefferson Street.

In December, 1883 the Spokane Methodist College opened on College Avenue (one block south of Broadway) and Jefferson Street. Founded by Col. David P. Jenkins, attorney and philanthropist, the college was short-lived, closing in May, 1892. However, the street still bears the name it received from the location of the school.

## 5. FIRST BRICK HOUSE ON THE NORTH SIDE, West 1843 Broadway Avenue.

Mel Grimmer, founder of Grimmer Transfer and Storage, built his home here 1886.

## 6. GLOVER'S LAST HOME, † N. 1408 Summit Boulevard.

In 1910 Uncle Jimmie built this cottage where he lived until his death in 1921.

## 7. WATER-MAIN BRIDGE across the Spokane River below Summit Blvd. and " Street.

Soldiers stationed at Fort George Wright used this footbridge to cross the river reach the end of the trolley line at Natatorium Park. (Nat Park was located down the at the west end of Boone Avenue along the river. A mobile home park occupies the s now.) Water pipes cross the bridge now owned by the Spokane Water Department supply the Ft. Wright area with city water.

## 8. A typical K.K. CUTTER-DESIGNED HOME, 1910, stands at 1715 West Po Road. (West Point Road lies high above the banks of the Spokane River at the west end Mission Avenue.)

**60**

## 9. WILLIAM PETTET'S "GLASGOW LODGE," 1735 West Point Road.

This home is possibly the oldest, continuously lived-in house in Spokane. It is thought that the property was originally homesteaded by a Civil War veteran who put up a slab hut around 1872. It's not certain what happened next, but by March 7, 1883, William Maxwell had established residence here. Then William Pettet acquired the property in 1889, remodeling it to resemble a former home in Bermuda. Pettet was successful in real estate in Spokane as well as being one of the organizers of the Edison Electric Illuminating Company in 1887. This was the forerunner of Washington Water Power.

After Pettet's death in 1904, Garner Chamberlin bought the property from the estate of his uncle's widow, Carolyn Pettet, and in turn sold it to his brother Theodore. In 1944 Roy Hathaway bought it from Theodore Chamberlin. Two years later Col. George S. Clarke, a grandson of A.M. Cannon, purchased the property. According to Mrs. Clarke, the original part of the house was the present (1962) sunroom, bathroom, and study. The log walls have been enclosed so no visible evidence of their location remains. Col. Clarke died in 1968.

## 10. THE CASTLE, northwest end of Rimrock Drive. (It can easily be seen looking across the river toward the Rimrock area from Northwest Boulevard and Providence Avenue.)

B.M. FRANCIS (for whom Francis Avenue was named) opened a real estate office in Spokane in 1907, already having real estate interests in Butte and Missoula, Montana. He platted subdivisions in all three cities. Although he had acquired a fortune in other transactions, his plans for Castle Hill on Rimrock Drive did not materialize. When he built his own home at the far northwest end of Rimrock Drive, it was considered quite a showplace. Eventually, it became too expensive to maintain, and he gave it up. For twenty years it stood empty, then served briefly as a dinner and night club. In recent years it is again a private home.

## 11. BOWL AND PITCHER, Riverside State Park.

These basalt formations in the Spokane River were created about ten million years ago during the Miocene Era. In 1935 this area became a part of the State Park system. Camping, picnicking, and hiking facilities are available.

Hours: May - Oct. 15, 8 a.m. - 10 p.m.; the rest of the year: 8 a.m. - 5 p.m. No entrance fee; camping: $5.50 per night.

Follow Summit Boulevard, keeping to the left onto West Point Road and downhill along Pettet Drive. Follow the river along Downriver Drive until one reaches Riverside State Park. From other locations one can use Northwest Boulevard, turning southwest onto Meenach Drive to Downriver Drive; or take Francis Avenue west, which will turn right onto Nine Mile Road. At the Spokane Rifle Club turn left. It will lead to the Aubrey L. White Parkway. Left again, following upstream to the Bowl and Pitcher area.)

## 12. ST. GEORGE'S SCHOOL, W. 2929 Waikiki Road.

(From the Bowl and Pitcher follow the directions above, reversing to Nine Mile Road. Continue northwest on Nine Mile Road to Nine Mile Falls. Here take a hard right uphill onto Rutter Parkway. Follow it past the Indian Painted Rocks to Waikiki Road.)

This private school is located on the Louis C. Davenport estate along the Little Spokane River. Davenport's home, "Flowerfield," 1928, is part of the campus.

## 13. WAIKIKI RETREAT HOUSE

(From St. George's drive east on Waikiki Road to Mill Road, then north on Mill to Fairwood Drive. Turn left.)

In 1911 Jay P. Graves sold his home at 2123 West First Avenue (Tour IX, No. 7) to Aubrey White and moved to the Selheim Springs area on the Little Spokane River. The property had been purchased from William E. Hall who had called it "Hallmere." Graves set about developing his thousand acres into a model farm and his gracious mansion into the finest country home in the northwest. His only son named it for the Hawaiian beach whose name fascinated him. In recent years the home has served as a Retreat House for Gonzaga University and the farm, including Fairwood Shopping Center, has long-since been subdivided.

(Return on Mill Road turning left at the Y onto Waikiki Road which in turn becomes North Wall. Continue south on wall to Garland Avenue, then east to Lidgerwood Street.)

## 14. ST. DAVID'S ESPISCOPAL CHURCH, 1892, southeast corner of Garland Avenue and Lidgerwood Street.

Built of native stone, this charming church is one of the oldest church buildings in Spokane. It was built for the Episcopal Church, but other denominations have used it since.

## 15. PRICE HOME, East 1427 Gordon, 1893.

This was a mining magnate's mansion. It is one of the few homes that has a stained glass window in the chimney.

## 16. WEST 908 FREDERICK AVENUE, northwest corner of Frederick and Lincoln Street.

A Coeur d'Alene man by the name of Leary built this house in 1887 for his bride-to-be, but she ran away with a "drummer," so . . . he sold the house! Robert W. Forrest, first mayor of Spokane Falls, was the purchaser. He added the turret so he could watch the horse races at Corbin Park.

## 17. CORBIN PARK, "The fastest track west of the Mississippi."

(Corbin Park is located between Waverly Place and Park Place at the foot of the North Hill. Post Street from the north side or Washington from the south are the best routes for reaching it.)

In March of 1887 the citizens of Spokane Falls subscribed to a $5000 fund for the purchase and construction of a horse race track. By September a one-half mile track with a 30-stall stable was completed at the foot of the north hill, east of Monroe. A grandstand fair buildings and other structures were built also. This first fairgrounds and race track opened in the fall of 1887. Sometimes a baseball game would be held in the center of the track as an added attraction, one inning being played between each race. On other occasions a pistol shooting contest provided extra entertainment.

When the fairgrounds and race track moved to other locations, the land was sold D.C. Corbin, who platted the area for housing. However, the old race track, remained Corbin Park.

## 18. MUSEUM OF NATIVE AMERICAN CULTURE, East 200 Cataldo.

(From Boone Avenue turn south on N. Gorp Street which will lead one to the Museum.)

This excellent Indian Museum was established in 1966 by the Reverend W.P. Schoenberg, S.J., Jerome Peltier and Richard T. Lewis for the promotion of Indian studies and the preservation of Indian cultures. It is well worth seeing. Guided tours are available and should be arranged for the optimum enjoyment of the exhibits. Gift shop.

(Hours: Tues. - Sat.: 8:30 a.m. - 4:30 p.m.; Sunday summer hours: 12 - 4:30 p.m. May - Labor Day. Nominal entrance fee.)

## 19. JAMES MONAGHAN, 1902, East 217 Boone Avenue.

Gonzaga University's Music Conservatory occupies this fine, old 14-room home. The exterior is solid brick with a cement coating, while the interior features heavy oak doors with bead trim. Monaghan, who first came into the Spokane country in the 1860s, was a financier associated with mining interests and railroad building. (See Tour II, No. 10) While at LaPray Bridge, Monaghan planted the first apple trees in the county.

The Monaghan's son, John Robert, was born in Chewelah March 26, 1873, and became one of the first twenty scholars at Gonzaga College which had been established by the Jesuit Fathers in 1887. (See Tour VIII, No. 28, for the rest of the story about John.)

Monaghan Home on West Boone, 1902 (Gonzaga University Music Department)

## 0. GONZAGA UNIVERSITY, East Boone Avenue.

Father Joseph Cataldo bought 320 acres (south of Mission Avenue and east of Division Street) from the Northern Pacific Railroad October 13, 1881, for the site of an Indian school. However, upon the petition from the city for a college, and to forestall a Methodist one, Fr. Cataldo concurred. Work was slow, but classes finally began September 17, 1887. By 1894 Gonzaga was incorporated into an academic college and conferred Bachelor of Arts Degrees for the first time.

Located originally at Pearl Street and DeSmet Avenue, the college building was moved to DeSmet and Astor Street, behind today's St. Aloysius Church. The Administration Building at 502 East Boone Avenue was completed in 1899 and expanded in 1903.

63

### 21. BING CROSBY'S BOYHOOD HOME, E. 508 Sharp.

Born in Tacoma, WA, Bing grew up in Spokane, attending Gonzaga Prep and Gonzaga University. The University purchased the home on the southeast corner of Sharp and Addison for an Alumni Center.

### 22. JUDGE NASH HOME, East 1624 South Riverton.

One of the features of this home is the curved glass library windows. From its location (South Riverton fronts the long curve of the Spokane River north from East Mission and across the bridge east of the Washington Water Power building), the house dominated the land between the Mission and Greene Street Bridges.

### 23. IRON HORSE.

This 1904 Union Pacific Railroad steam locomotive is on display at the Spokane Interstate Fairgrounds which is located on North Havana Street and East Broadway Avenue.

(Drive east on Mission Avenue to Havana Street, then south.)

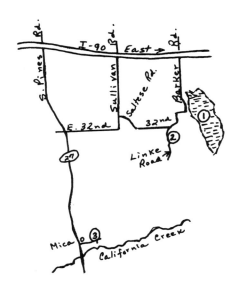

## PART C

### 1. SALTESE LAKE.

(Take the Barker Road exit south from I-90.)

Saltese lake was located just west of the Holidays Hills Recreation Center. In area it was larger than Liberty lake, but being quite shallow, it was drained about 1894. The valley of the Spokane River to the Falls was called the Coeur d'Alene Prairie on Mullan's and other early maps because this was the home territory of the Coeur d'Alene Indians. Chief Andrew Seltice lived near Saltese Lake. The Coeur d'Alenes shared the fare with the Upper Spokans who lived north of the river on Peone Prairie.

**COURCHAINE HOUSE,** South Linke Road.

Daniel Courchaine, born in Winnipeg, came to the Spokane area in 1866 and bought his land from the Indians in 1867. He put up some log buildings in which he and his family lived until this house was finished in 1878. It took a year for him to haul the lumber from Walla Walla, the closest sawmill. The outside of the house has changed little. To the east of the house is a stone shed with two-foot walls which probably was built before the house. Other buildings on this farm included a tool shed, bunk house, grainery, two horse barns, chicken house and the well-known outhouse. All that remains now in addition to the house is the big barn built in 1889 and the little brick well or milk house (1880s) with a natural spring cooling system.

(One-half mile south of 32nd Avenue on the east side of Linke Road is the white house with red trim.)

**CALIFORNIA RANCH,** † California Creek, Mica, WA.

California Ranch was frequently referred to by early settlers in the Spokane country. It is believed some of the land was plowed as early as 1864. The Kentuck Trail (see epilogue) passed by. In 1867 a fellow by the name of Henry Lueg kept a journal while traveling from Minnesota to Oregon in an emigrant party. From Spokane Bridge they followed the Kentuck Trail to Walla Walla as it was shorter than the Mullan Road.

Lueg mentioned a farm (Courchaine's) seven miles from the bridge and California Ranch five miles further on. A store and farm were at the crossing of the Palouse River, but these were the only settlers between Spokane Bridge and the Snake River Ferry.

One of the emigrants, Peter Dueber, sold a wagon at California Ranch. Perhaps this was to Knight, who sold his squatter's rights to Maxim Mullouin (Mulwine) in 1871.

(Take the road east through Mica from State Highway 27 [South Pines Road]. Less than a mile the road turns south, right at the big barn of California Ranch.)

Although no records remain, it is likely the big barn was built during the 1870s or 80s. It was made of hand-hewn timbers with a field stone foundation. This land has been continuously farmed, making it probably the oldest ranch in Spokane County.

# PART D — NEARBY PLACES

**HALLETT'S CASTLE,** † 1900, East 623 Lake Street, Medical Lake, WA

Stanley Hallett came from London and eventually settled at Medical Lake. There he built his "castle," the grounds of which also included a tennis court, an ice house, a large barn and a grape arbor. Solid granite two to three feet thick formed the foundation of the house. On the third floor was a ballroom complete with a kitchen. The grand piano which had been shipped around the horn, had to be hoisted to the third floor before the stairs were put in. It became a tradition for the townspeople to gather on the lawn at dusk on the Fourth of July to watch the fireworks. Hallett provided $50 worth which were set off from the Castle's tower. Hallett served Medical Lake as its first mayor in 1900. This home is now subdivided into 11 apartments.

(Take Exit 272 off I-90; Medical Lake Road. Follow the Silver Lake sign into town which is Lefevre Stree Turn east (left) onto Lake Street. The Hallett House, a three-story, red brick, is on the north side of Lake St 6 blocks from Lefevre.)

**Hallett's Castle, Medical Lake.**

## 2. SUTTON'S RED BARN, † Cheney, Washington.

Built in 1884, this large barn was originally a horse barn, double-walled and pegg (no nails). It received its name from one of the owners who was a state senator. Locate just off Washington Street on the western edge of Eastern Washington University Campu this landmark houses offices for the university.

## 3. CHENEY DEPOT, † 505 Second Street, Cheney, Washington.

This depot served as the southern terminal for the Interurban Electric Railway th Washington Water Power operated between Spokane and Cheney until the 1920s.

## 4. TURNBULL NATIONAL WILDLIFE REFUGE.

Over 200 different kinds of birds inhabit this wildlife refuge as well as mammals a smaller animals. A display pond by the refuge headquarters features trumpeter swar geese, ducks and other water birds. There is a four-mile self-guiding auto tour, hiki trails, picnic area and rest area. There are no facilities for food, lodging or camping. T area closes at dark.

(Turnbull is located four miles south of Cheney on the Cheney-Plaza Road (Badger Lake Road), then 2 miles on the entrance road. Take binoculars. Note: The mosquitoes are very friendly.)

## 5. DYBDALL GRIST MILL, † 1898.

Where Rock Creek empties into the south end of Chapman Lake stands t dilapidated remains of an old grist mill. Built by Ole Dybdall, a Norwegian immigr; from Seattle, it ground wheat into flour for the area farmers. His son continued operati until 1950, making this one of the last custom grist mills in the Pacific Northwest. currently runs a resort just up the road from the mill.

(Continue south on the Cheney-Plaza Road for another 6 miles to Chapman Lake. A fishing resort is on the ( of the lake, the mill just south, fenced, and the grass surrounding is used for pasture.)

# AREAS

From time to time one reads or hears of areas in Spokane referred to by name, which can be confusing. The following are a few:

**1. BROWNE'S ADDITION,** the residential section west of downtown Spokane bordered by Maple Street, Sunset Highway, the bluffs of Hangman Creek and the Spokane River. This was the original homestead of J.J. Browne, emigrant of 1878 and one of the promoters and developers of early Spokan Falls. (See map, Tour IX.)

**2. CANNON HILL,** primarily the area directly south of downtown and south of Browne's Addition. It was part of A.M. Cannon's homestead, who also came in 1878, opened the first bank in Spokan Falls and was a well-known entrepreneur.

**3. DEEP CREEK,** two miles west of Fairchild Air Base at the foot of a steep hill on U.S. Highway 2. For a tour of the Deep Creek area, see Peggy Bal's *Fairchild—Heritage of the Spokane Plains*, p. 85.

**. ROSS PARK,** a fashionable residential area of the 1890s, on the northwest side of the Spokane River running from Perry to Crestline Street and from the riverbank to the Great Northern Railroad tracks (now Burlington-Northern). The first street electric railway which ran the 4½ miles from downtown to Ross Park began service November 17, 1889. The Washington Water Power Building and grounds now cover a large part of this addition.

**. UNION PARK,** roughly an irregular area of residences lying below Altamont Boulevard beginning at Third Avenue and between Magnolia and Regal Streets. Jim Glover traversed this area when he first came to the settlement by the falls. The only road from the east followed the old Mullan Road to Moran Prairie. It then turned northwest for five miles, being not much more than a make-shift road that went over the steep and rocky basaltic bluff to the flat by the river at what became Union Park.

**. VINEGAR FLAT,** a colloquial nickname referring to the flat of land between Inland Empire Way and Hangman Creek, and from West 10th Avenue to 16th Avenue or so. From 1890-1958 the Keller-Lorenz Vinegar Works operated in a three-story brick building at 11th Avenue and Spruce Street on the banks of the creek. Cider, malt and white wine vinegar were produced. Pieces of red brick and some cement floor remain at the site.

About 10th Avenue was the old swimming hole in the creek. A former resident tells of the times in the early part of the century when the Cannon (Hill) "Bullies" came down the bluff to swim. Invariably there would be a fight with the local boys. Too young to participate, he hid in the bushes and watched! Another favorite pasttime was catching large crayfish (the size of crabs) and boiling them for a feast on the beach.

Jim Stafford was the original homesteader, and the area is better known by his name today.

# Map of Early Roads in Washington

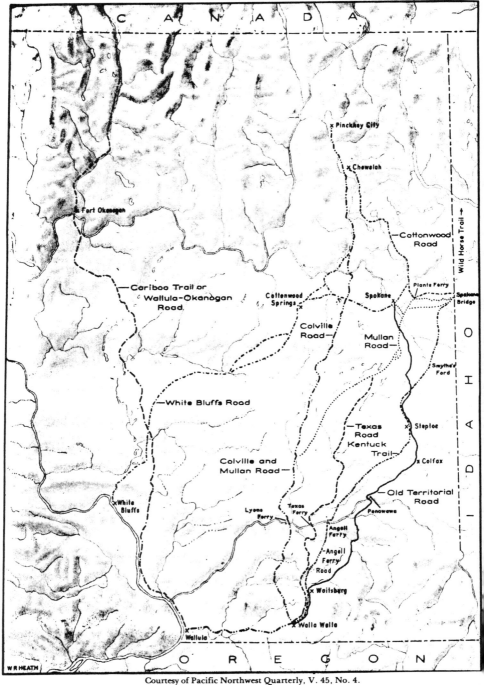

# EPILOGUE — TRAILS AND OLD ROADS

Wagon wheels and plodding hooves carved out the early roads following the terrain of least resistance. They went where there were grass and water for the animals and where the grades down to and up from creeks and streams and rivers were the most gradual. They tried to avoid swamps, lakes, rocky ground and dense forests. At best, frontier roads were hazardous, rough and bumpy. Fifteen miles a day was a good average with a loaded wagon. And yet these tracks and ruts in the ground often developed into parts of our current highways. Although we travel at a greater speed and with much more comfort — no dust, sweating bodies, sticky flies or stinging mosquitoes — we frequently see much the same scenery as those travelers of a century ago.

It is to be noted that all these roads or trails (except the Colville-Walla Walla Road) developed **after** Wright's treaty with the Palouse, Spokans and Coeur d'Alenes whereby the Indians promised that all white people could travel through their lands unmolested. Wright's treaty was perhaps far more reaching than even he realized.

## 1. COLVILLE-WALLA WALLA ROAD.

This was the oldest road in our area and developed from Indian trails. Beginning at old Fort Walla Walla (Wallula, on the north side of the confluence of the Walla Walla and Columbia Rivers), it followed the Walla Walla River east to the present city by that name. There it turned north to the Lyons Ferry crossing of the Snake River at the mouth of the Palouse River. (A bridge has been built at this ferry site which had operated continuously since 1859.) Keeping west of the Palouse River, the road continued northward following Cow Creek to its source in Sprague Lake. After passing along the east side of Sprague Lake, there was a stop-over and watering hole at Willow Springs. Still traveling northward the road came within five miles west of Deep Creek and passed over Coulee Creek at its forks. The Spokane River was crossed at the LaPray Bridge location (Tour II, No. 10). From there it followed Chamokane Creek valley north to Colville.

Traders at Spokane House followed an Indian trail along the north bank of the Spokane River downstream to reach this Colville Trail. The Walkers and Eells of Tshimakain Mission used this route which ran past their homes to go to Fort Colvile for supplies.

Following the Wright campaign, this route was used as a military road in 1859 for the newly established Fort Colville and Pinkney City (Tour II, No. 3). A surprising amount of freight was carried to Pinkney City. In 1864 a wagon train of six-mule teams hauled 40,000 pounds of merchandise in one trip — and made six trips during the season. Freight costs were high, creating the following prices: coffee—75¢ a pound, sugar—50¢, salt—25¢, nails—40¢, shot—50¢, and a spool of thread or a packet of needles—25¢.

## MULLAN ROAD, 1859-1862.

Much has been written of this military road (Tour III, No. 9; Tour IV, No. 1; and Tour V, No. 6.) whose engineer accompanied Col. Wright on his campaign. That expedition gave Mullan a chance to look over the first part of the journey. The Mullan Road followed the Colville-Walla Walla Road as far as Cow Creek, 25 miles north of the Snake River. From there it turned northeast.

In Spokane County it passed east of Chapman Lake, across the Stubblefield Lake area of Turnbull National Wildlife Refuge, skirted the rim of Philleo Lake and traversed Paradise Prairie between Cheney and Spangle. The first year the Mullan Road crossed Hangman Creek at Smythe's Ford (Tour IV, No. 2) and went south of Coeur d'Alene Lake. But this way proved to be too wet, so a northern route was developed.

In 1867 the Washington Territorial Legislature authorized one Patrick Farrell to build and keep a toll bridge across Hangman Creek on the direct road from Walla Walla to Fort Benton. Which was—where? Dr. C.S. Kingston, Professor of History, Eastern Washington University, who did a great deal of research on pioneer roads of the Inland Empire, said the Mullan Road crossed Hangman Creek in Section 16, township 24 N Range 43 EWM, continuing on about 3 miles to the northwest corner of section 2 of the same townshp where a road branched off and led to Spokan Falls five miles away.

Translating that as closely as possible to the Hangman Valley Road, it comes out about 1½ miles east of the turn-off from South Hatch Road. Climbing up the banks of the north side of the creek, the road crossed Moran Prairie and made a fairly straight run to Plante's Ferry. In 1867 it used Schnebley's Bridge to cross the Spokane River.

Once through the Coeur d'Alene Mountains the road from Missoula passed north of Helena, through Great Falls to its completion at Fort Benton on the Missouri River. Mullan described the road as: the first 180 miles in open prairie, level or rolling; the next 120 mountain stream bottoms, densely wooded; next 224 miles open timbered plateau with long stretches of prairie, and the last 100 level or rolling prairie.

The road from Walla Walla to Spokane Bridge was used a great deal, as was the eastern end over the prairies. The section through the mountains, however, didn't fare very well By 1877 the road had become clogged by washouts, windfalls, etc. When Generals P.H. Sheridan and W.T. Sherman made an inspection trip to the West that summer, they reported that part of the Mullan Road had been reduced through neglect to a mere pack trail and had not been traveled by wagons for years.

Nevertheless, the success of Mullan's judgment through the Coeur d'Alene Mountains and into Montana is evidenced in the location of U.S. highways and railroads which closely followed the path he laid out.

## 3. CARIBOO TRAIL, 1859-1868.

The mines in British Columbia enticed thousands of would-be prospectors to cross the international border *via* the Okanogan Valley. From Wallula this route followed the east side of the Columbia River to Ringold where it swung northeast. It stayed southeast Othello, slightly east of Warden, Moses Lake and Wheeler before turning northwest toward Sun Lakes. The Columbia River was crossed near Coulee City and again at Fort Okanogan (1811-1860) where the Okanogan River joins the Columbia. From there the route shadowed the Okanogan River north into British Columbia and the Cariboo mining district, the final destination—Barkerville.

Then came the discovery of gold in Montana which hastened the need for the shortest possible routes. Several new roads were developed.

## 4. WHITE BLUFFS ROAD, 1860-1870.

The Oregon Steam Navigation Company wanted to promote Portland trade in the western Montana gold fields and its own freight service as the carrier. So, a depot consisting of warehouses and a supervisor's home was built on the White Bluffs of the

olumbia River, 50 miles north of Wallula. This was about as far north as the steam boats
uld go. Here the freight was unloaded and sent overland. The route went north over the
addle Mountains and Frenchmen Hills, Keeping east of Moses Lake, it swung northeast
• Odessa on Crab Creek. Continuing northeast there was a stop at Cottonwood Springs
resent site of Davenport), then eastward (U.S. 2 follows this section) past Reardan, Deep
reek and across lower Hangman Creek at Riverside Avenue (Tour X, No. 11). It used the
neaquoteen Crossing at LaClede over the Pend Oreille River. The road ended at the
eamboat landing at the lower end of Pend Oreille Lake where the goods were transferred
lake steamers. They were then boated to Cabinet Gorge on the Clark Fork River. Plans
lled for two river steamers: one to operate as far as Thompson Falls and the second to
ork the upper river beyond the falls.

Ambitious as this plan was, it was short-lived, as there was soon freight wagon service
nnecting the Union Pacific Railroad from Utah to Montana. Furthermore, freighters
referred to go to Walla Walla City for more "life," and the mines petered out in a short
ne.

The White Bluffs Road was also the shortest distance to Colville from the Columbia
ver, and some freight was hauled this way. Near Reardan the route turned north to tie
with the Colville-Walla Walla Road.

## KENTUCK TRAIL, 1864-1872.

Basically, the Kentuck Trail was the most direct route from Walla Walla to Spokane
idge on the way to the Montana gold diggings. It received its name from colorful Joe
entuck" Ruark, one of the proprietors of the Blackfoot Ferry across the Snake River.

The 1864-1865 Territorial Legislature authorized Thomas W. Davidson to establish
erry on the Snake River at the Indian crossing of "Y-Youks-ber-nets." Davidson later
med a partnership with Ruark. Knowing that lots of eager miners would be heading for
 placer gold mines on the Little Blackfoot River in western Montana, they called their
terprise by that name. To entice business they advertised their Blackfoot Ferry in the
alla Walla *Statesmen* as being the shortest route (15 miles shorter than the Mullan
ad), with good grass, water and wood for camping. From Walla Walla the road ran
out as straight as one could go, crossing the Touchet at Waitsburg and the Tucannon
d Pataha near their confluence at Platter's crossing. This section south of the Snake was
own as the Angell Ferry Road.

From the north side of the Snake, the Kentuck Trail traversed Union Flat (renamed
m Confederate), forded the Palouse 14 miles west of Colfax, and went through Pleasant
lley and Cottonwood. Thorn Creek was crossed a mile below Thornton. From there to
salia the old U.S. 195 followed the same route. Still keeping to a northeast direction, the
d passed north of Spring Valley, and crossed Hangman Creek at Smyth's Ford (Tour
, No. 2). It continued on through Mount Hope, Freeman, and one mile east of Mica
 California Ranch, Tour IX, Part C, No. 3) to Spokane Bridge.

From the Spangle-Waverly Road, the county road bearing north across Hangman
ek to the Valley Chapel-Mt. Hope Road still bears the name: North Kentuck Trails.

## WILD HORSE TRAIL, 1864-1880.

While some roads were deliberately built, this one just "happened." Again, it was the
 of the siren gold that lured men north, this time to the Wild Horse Creek near Fort
ele, British Columbia.

71

The top two-thirds of the trail—from the Kootenay River through Cranbrook, pa Moyie Lake and along the Moyie River valley to Bonner's Ferry, then down the Ida panhandle to Lake Pend Oreille—was originally traveled by the Kootenais and oth Indian tribes. This was the route taken by David Thompson in 1808, Governor Simpson the Hudson's Bay Company in 1841, and approximates U.S. Highway 95 from t Canadian border.

From Sandpoint south the trail was more contemporary, dating from the surveyi activities of the U.S. Boundary Commission in 1859. The easiest way from Sandpoint w southwest along the Pend Oreille River to the Seneaquoteen Ford. From the Hoodoo Val with a veer to the southeast to bypass Hoodoo Lake, the trail jogged southwest again Westwood (Rathdrum) and hence to Spokane Bridge. To travel further south o followed the Mullan Road or Kentuck Trail.

In March of 1864 gold had been found on Wild Horse Creek, and by June 500 m had arrived. At the height of the rush over 20,000 men were in the area. All of the people needed food and supplies. The major supply point was Walla Walla, only 408 mi distant as compared to 500 miles to Hope, B.C. The shorter distance and easier tra developed the Wild Horse Trail. The boom was over by 1880.

## 7. TEXAS ROAD, 1865-1880.

This road was an exception. In most instances ferries were built to accommo roads, but in this case the ferry came first. Three partners: Jesse Thompson, T.M. Slocu and Thomas Newlon built a ferry across the Snake River at Riparia in 1865, about 5 m upstream from the mouth of the Tucannon. It was one of the longest-lived ferries ac thé Snake. However, in order to get customers to use the ferry, a road was needed. Hen the Texas Road, actually an extension of the ferry, came into being.

After reaching the Palouse tableland north of the Snake, the road ran northeas miles to Schreck, north to LaCrosse and then northwest to the Palouse River. Here it necessary to build a bridge near the mouth of Rock Creek to make the Texas Road n attractive to travelers. After skirting Rock Lake on the west side, the route northeastward to the southern boundary of Spokane County where it fused with Mullan Road.

## 8. COTTONWOOD ROAD, 1867-1889.

Recognizing potential customers in the miners scurrying through Spokane Bri the ranchers in the Colville Valley built a 60-mile road to the bridge in 1887. Cut thro dense timber, the road followed Cottonwood Creek south of Chewelah, hence the nam passed Loon Lake and Deer Park, crossing the Little Spokane on a bridge soutl Chatteroy.

In 1881 the road was improved by detachments of soldiers from Ft. Colville. S this route was shorter to Colville from Spokane Falls than by way of LaPray Bridg continued to be the freighting road until D.C. Corbin's Spokane Falls & Nortl Railroad was built in 1889. U.S. Highway 395 closely parallels the route of the Cottonwood Road, but the location of the Burlington-Northern follows it more exa

## 9. OLD TERRITORIAL ROAD, 1872-

By 1872 there were enough settlers in eastern Washington to warrant the Territ government to authorize a road from Walla Walla City to Ft. Colville. It was to go by f Waitsburg and Bellville (Colfax), crossing the Snake River at Penawawa. Later a lower ossing at Central Ferry would be used. No money was appropriated for these territorial ads—that was the problem of each county's commissioners. Surveying began June 3, 372, and was completed at the Chatteroy bridge over the Little Spokane 26 days later.

From Colfax the route was *via* Steptoe, Thornton and Rosalia. Between the latter two wns it coincided with the Kentuck Trail. Then came Spangle and Hangman Creek. It is kely that the natural ford at 11th Avenue was used to cross Hangman. From there it gled up to the break in the bluff between 7th and 6th Avenues, the route of the railroads d Inland Empire Way. After crossing the Spokane River at the falls, the road continued rth to Chattaroy where it tied in with the Cottonwood Road to Ft. Colville.

Basically, U.S. 195 approximates this old Territorial Road, which was used by many Spokane's earliest settlers.

## 1. SPOKANE FALLS — COLVILLE ROAD, late 1870s.

As frequently happened, this wagon road followed an old Indian trail from the Big lls to the Little Falls on the Spokane River. There are tracks in the Seven Mile-Deep eek area still clearly evident. Some of the old property deeds are described as being on e Colville Road. The Old Trails Road west of Ft. Wright and running northward is very :ely part of this past route of travel.

riving west on Seven Mile Road, turn south on Inland Road for 1½ miles. Turn right on the first road for .3 of a te. This dead-ends at Old Trails. Turn right and follow the road down to its crossing over Deep Creek. One can ntinue walking up the grade across the creek bottom or proceed by car back to Seven Mile Road, then west one te. Park. The land on the left is Riverside State Park land. Follow the dirt road about 700 feet, then walk under trees to the right 40 feet. There you will find five or more sets of tracks which could have been used by teams ng downhill yielding to a heavily-laden wagon coming up the main road.)

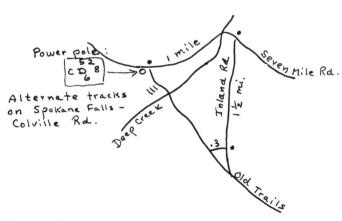

## INLAND EMPIRE HIGHWAY.

The first modern highway reaching Spokane from the south was the Palouse hway. Now it's the "Old" Palouse Highway or the "scenic" route as it winds back and h from Pullman to Palouse, through Oakesdale, Tekoa, Fairfield, Rockford, :man, Valleyford and over Glenrose Prairie to east Spokane. It was built about 1910.

By 1914 a faster, straighter route was needed between Spokane and Colfax, and the nd Empire Highway came into being. The cost was a little less than two hundred thousand dollars, although the surfacing between Spangle and Rosalia was no more than gravel.

Twenty-five years later (1939) a "new" four-lane highway was constructed south of Spokane for 1.4 miles to eliminate a sharp, hairpin curve. In order to avoid building two bridges over Latah Creek, they simply changed the stream bed to run along the east side of the new road. By so doing, a big loop of the creek was amputated. From High Drive the old stream bed can be seen to the southwest, often filled with water, but with nowhere to go.

Loop of Hangman Creek, cut off in 1939.

# BIBLIOGRAPHY

skman, Allegra. Taped Oral History Interview with C. Hubert Bartoo, Eastern Washington State Historical Society, 1976.

al, Peggy. *Fairchild—Heritage of Spokane Plains.* 1976.

ean, Margaret. "Age of Elegance." Eastern Washington State Historical Society, 1968.

_____. "Campbell House." Eastern Washington State Historical Society, 1965.

echer, E.T. *Spokane Corona.* C.W.Hill, 1974.

ond, Rowland. *Early Birds in the Northwest.* Spokane House Enterprises, 1975.

oleman, Louis C. and Leo Rieman. *Mullan Road.* B.C. Payette, Montreal, 1968.

ullenty, Jim. "The Castle." *Spokane Daily Chronicle,* December 25, 1969.

urham, N.W. *History of the City of Spokane and Spokane County, Washington.* Vol. I, II, III, S.J. Clarke Pub. Co., 1912.

dwards, Jonathan. *History of Spokane County.* W.H. Lever, 1900.

Hult, Ruby. *Steamboats in the Timber.* Caxton, Caldwell, ID, 1952.

argo, Lucille F. *Spokane Story.* The Northwestern Press, Minneapolis, 1957.

reeman, Otis W. "Early Wagon Roads in the Inland Empire." *Pacific Northwest Quarterly,* Vol. 45, No. 4, 1954, October, pp. 125-130.

listory of the Electric Industry in Spokane and the Inland Empire." 1959, manuscript by Washington Water Power Co.

yslop, Robert B. *Spokane's Building Blocks.* Standard Blue Print Co., Inc., Spokane, WA, 1983.

ssett, Thomas E. *Chief Spokan Garry.* T.S. Denison & Co., Minneapolis, MN, 1960.

alez, Jay J. *Saga of a Western Town . . . Spokane.* Lawton Printing, Spokane, 1972.

_____. *This Town of Ours . . . Spokane.* Lawton Printing, Spokane, 1973.

ngston, Dr. C.S. "Northern Overland Route in 1867." Journal of Henry Lueg, *The Pacific Northwest Quarterly,* Vol. 41, No. 3, 1950, July, p. 248.

_____. "Pioneer Roads of This Region." *The Spokesman Review,* July 1, 15, 29; August 12, 26, 1951.

zer, Benjamin H. "Michael M. Cowley." *The Pacific Northwesterner,* Vol. 9, No. 2, 1965, Spring, pp. 25-31.

owrach, Rev. Edward J. *Big Bend Missions and Medical Lake.* 1963.

rd, John Keast. *The Naturalist in Vancouver Island and British Columbia.* Vol 2, London, 1866.

agnuson, Richard G. *Coeur d'Alene Diary.* Metropolitan Press, Portland, 1968.

ltier, Jerome A. "Neglected Spokane House." *The Pacific Northwesterner,* Vol. 5, No. 3, 1961, Summer, pp. 33-41.

_____. "Pinkney City." *The Pacific Northwesterner,* Vol. 7, No. 4, 1963, Fall, pp. 61-64.

_____. *Warbonnets and Epaulets.* Payette, Montreal, 1971.

eserving Washington's History.* Washington State Parks and Recreation Commission, 1976.

eston, R.N. *Early Washington.* Western Guide Pub., Corvallis, OR, 1974.

eminiscences of Pioneers in the Inland Empire." Wm. S. Lewis interview with Ben Norman, *The Spokesman Review,* Nov. 1, 1925.

eport of the Inspection Made in the Summer of 1877 by Generals P.H. Sheridan and W.T. Sherman." Washington, D.C., 1878.

oenberg Wilfred P., S.J. *Gonzaga University, 75 Years.* Lawton Printing Co., Spokane, WA, 1963.

rfey, Florence E. *Vanished Gristmills and the Men Who Ran Them.* Ye Galleon Press, Fairfield, 1978.

mble, Louis. "The Wild Horse Trail." *The Spokesman Review,* Nov. 30, 1952.

ashington State Historical Quarterly.* Vol. VII, No. 1, (Jan. 1916).

necoop, David C. *Children of the Sun.* Wellpinit, 1969.

**CKNOWLEDGEMENTS:**

s. Elinor Kelly, former Librarian, Eastern Washington State Historical Society; Spokane Public Library; ome A. Peltier and Father Edward J. Kowrach, Authors and Researchers; Glen Adams, Publisher.

# Index

Albeni Falls ............................ 13
Angell Ferry Road ..................... 71
Army Officers' Quarters ............... 36, 38
Astor, John Jacob ...................... 10

Baer, Harry ........................ 47, 48
Bal, Peggy ............................. 67
Bartoo, George A. ..................... 40
Bassett Cabin .................... 25, 36, 41
Bassett, Chester Wilbur ............... 25
Bassett, Herman Sherman ............. 25
Bassett, Minnie Maria ............ 25, 26, 40
Bassett Spring ................... 22, 25, 26
Bassett, Wilbur Fiske ............... 25, 40
Bates, J.T. ............................ 16
Battle of Four Lakes ................ 22, 25
Battle of Spokane Plains ............ 22, 26
Bean, Margaret ........................ 49
Bellevue Hotel ........................ 44
Bennett Block ..................... 36, 46
Big Falls .............................. 73
Blackfoot Ferry ....................... 71
Bon Marche, The ...................... 46
Brick Streets ......................... 58
Brodie Block ...................... 36, 45
Browne, J.J. .............. 51, 52, 53, 67
Browne's Addition ...... 34, 45, 49, 55, 58, 67
Bunker Hill & Sullivan Mine ......... 48

C & C Flour Mill ............... 36, 40, 41
California House ...... 36, 37, 38, 44, 48, 58
California Ranch .................... 65, 71
Camp Washington .................... 8, 11
Campbell, Amasa B. ................... 52
Campbell House ....................... 52
Cannon, A.M. .......... 46, 51, 53, 61, 67
Cannon Hill .......................... 67
Cariboo Trail ...................... 68, 70
Carousel ........................... 36, 38
Carpenter, W.J. ...................... 51
Cataldo, Father Joseph ......... 18, 19, 63
Catholic Chancery ................. 36, 42
Castle, The .......................... 61
Cave, Post Falls ..................... 27
Chamber of Commerce Bldg. .......... 42
Chamberlain, Garner .................. 61
Chamberlain, Theodore ............... 61
Cheney Depot ......................... 66
Chinese Cemetery .................... 52
City Hall ................. 41, 42, 44, 48
Clark, Dennis ........................ 53

Clark, F. Lewis ................ 40, 55, 5
Clark, James ......................... 5
Clark, Patrick F. .................... 5
Clarke, Col. George S. ............... 6
Clough, Charles ...................... 3
Coeur d'Alene Hotel ........... 36, 47, 4
Colvile, Andrew .................... 10, 1
Colville-Walla Walla Rd. ...... 8, 11, 15, 1
    68, 69, 71
Commercial Hotel ..................... 4
Corbet, James V. ..................... 5
Corbin, Austin ....................... 5
Corbin, D.C. ............... 51, 56, 62, 7
Corbin House ......................... 5
Corbin, Mary ......................... 5
Cottonwood Road ................ 68, 72, 
Coulee Creek ....................... 11, 
Courchaine, Daniel ................... 
Cowles, W.H. ....................... 43, 
Cowley, Michael M. ................ 29, 
Cowley House ......................... 
Cowley, Rev. H.T. .............. 9, 29, 
Crawford, W.H. ....................... 
Crescent Building .................... 
Crosby, Bing ......................... 
Curtis, Frank E. .................... 40, 
Cutter, Corbin ....................... 
Cutter, Horace ....................... 
Cutter, Kirtland K. ................ 42, 
    49-56, 60

Davenport, Louis ................... 44, 
Davenport "Flowerfield" .............. 
Davenport Hotel ..................... 36, 
Davenport Restaurant ............... 36, 
Davidson, Thomas W. .................. 
Davis, George A. ..................... 
Davis, James H. "Cashup" ............. 
Dead-End Alleys .................... 36, 
Deep Creek ..................... 63, 67, 71
DeSmet, Father Peter J. .............. 
Dill, Senator Clarence C. ............ 
Downing, John J. ..................... 37
Drumheller Springs ................. 8, 9
Dueber, Peter ........................ 
Duffy & Butler's Saloon ............ 36
Durheim, Mrs. ........................ 
Dwight, Daniel ....................... 
Dwight House ......................... 
Dybdal Grist Mill .................... 
Dybdal, Ole ..........................

**489 Building** ....................... 36, 45
astern Washington State Historical
Society .......................... 51, 52
astern Washington University ......... 66, 70
ells, Rev. Cushing ............... 14, 15, 69
ells, Myra ...................... 14, 69
cho Flour Mill ................ 36, 39, 40
dison Electric Illuminating Company ...... 61
mpire State Building ................ 36, 43

**arrell, Patrick** ...................... 70
rnwell Building .................... 36, 45
nch Arboretum ..................... 50
nch, John A. ...................... 52
re Station No. 1 ............... 36, 45
re, The Spokane ......... 36, 40, 44, 45
rst Brick House on North Side ........... 60
rst Bridge ...................... 36, 39
rst House on North Side ............... 60
rst Store ....................... 37
ch, George ...................... 40
our Mill, The .................. 36, 40
rrest, Robert W. .................. 62
rts:
Benton ........................ 29, 70
Coeur d'Alene ...................... 28
Colvile (Fur Trading) ...... 10, 12, 14, 15, 69
Colville (Military) .......... 10, 12, 13, 69, 72
George Wright ...... 26, 30, 32, 33, 35, 60, 73
Okanogan ..................... 68, 70
Sherman ...................... 28
Spokane (Fur Trading) .............. 10
Spokane (Military) .............. 13, 32
Walla Walla ............. 24, 29, 68, 69
William (Fur Trading) ............... 9
rt Wright College of the Holy Names ...... 35
ur Corners ....................... 37
urth of July Canyon and Pass .......... 29
ancis, B.M. ...................... 61
ankfurt Block .................... 36, 47

**rden Springs** ...................... 34
rdner Cave ..................... 12, 13
rdner, Ed ...................... 13
rland, Hamlin ................... 46, 47
rry, See Spokan Garry
rry, Nina ..................... 34, 35
rmond Block .................. 36, 43
rmond, Eugene .................. 43
liam, Lane ..................... 38
ver & Gilliam Livery Stable ......... 36, 38
ver Field ............. 33, 34, 36, 41
ver Island .................... 38, 39
ver, James N. ........... 30, 34, 37, 39, 45, 47, 50, 51, 55, 60, 67

Glover, John ..................... 38, 48
Glover, Susan ..................... 45
Glover's Last Home ............... 60
Goetz, "Dutch" Jake ............. 47, 48
Goldsmith, August ................. 47
Gondola ...................... 36, 42
Gonzaga University ... 19, 30, 42, 62, 63, 64
Gordon, Burgess Lee ............. 55, 56
Goudy Grist Mill ................ 14
Graham's Hall .................. 36, 47
Grand Coulee Dam ............... 14
Grand Hotel .................... 46
Granite Curbs .................. 45, 46
Granite Lake ................... 25
Graves, Jay P. ................ 51, 62
Gray, Clara .................... 37
Gray Road ..................... 11
Gray, William C. ................. 37
Great Eastern Building
(Peyton) ..................... 36, 45
Great Northern Clock Tower .......... 36, 39
Great Western Building .............. 43
Greenwood Cemetery ................ 35
Greenwood House ............... 33, 35
Grimmer, Mel ................... 60

**Hall, William E.** .................. 62
Hallett's Castle ................ 65, 66
Hallett, Stanley ................. 65
Hangman Creek .............. 22, 24, 34, 63, 67, 70, 71, 73, 74
Hangman's Tree ................ 22, 23
Hathaway, Roy ................. 61
Havermale, Rev. Samuel G. .......... 39
Hill, Jim ..................... 58
Hitching Rings ............... 45, 60
Hogan Block ................... 45
Holland Block ................ 45, 52
Holly's Hardware ................ 47
Horse Slaughter Camp ........... 30, 31
Howard Street Bridge .............. 16
Hudson's Bay Company ...... 9, 10, 14, 72
Hunsaker's Grocery Store ......... 36, 38
Hussy, Warren .................. 51
Hutton, Levi and May ............. 29
Hyde, Rollin H. ................. 45
Hydroelectric Plant, Second ......... 36, 40

**Illim-Spokanee, Chief** ............. 9, 10
Indian Agency Building ........... 12, 14
Indian Canyon Creek and Falls ...... 19, 33, 34
Indian Caves .................. 12, 13
Indian Cemetery, Old ............ 17, 19
Indian Painted Rocks ............. 6, 8, 9, 27, 61

Indian Trail Road ....................8, 9
Inland Empire Highway ..................73
"Irish Kate" ..........................44
Iron Horse ...........................64

Jail, Early ........................36, 38
Jenkins, Col. David ....................60
Jones, Rolla A. .......................40
Junction of Riverside & Sprague
    at Cedar ...........................59

Kamiakin, Chief ......................24
Keller-Lorenz Vinegar Works ............67
Kellogg, Noah ........................48
Kentuck Trail ...........24, 65, 68, 71, 72, 73
Kettle Falls ......................10, 14
Kingston, Dr. C.S. ....................70
Knight, Mr. ..........................65
Kuhn, Aaron ......................45, 52
Kuhn Building ................36, 45, 52

Land Fill ......................36, 41, 42
Lane, Thaddeus S. .....................56
LaPray Bridge ...........12, 16, 63, 69, 72
LaPray, Joseph .........................16
Latah Creek ......................24, 74
Lee, Timothy .........................30
Levy Block ..........................45
Lewis, Richard T. .....................63
Liberty Lake .........................30
Lindsay, Vachel .......................52
Little Falls ....................12, 16, 73
Little Falls Dam .......................16
Little Red Chapel .................27, 28
Little Red Schoolhouse ...............33, 34
Loewenberg, Bernard ...............47, 51
Loewenberg, Herman ..................47
Log Building, Oldest .................1, 11
Log Cabin Saloon .....................43
Long Lake Camp & Picnic Area ..........15
Long Lake Dam .....................15, 16
Long Lake Pictographs .............12, 15
Long Lake Viewpoint ...............12, 15
Looff, Charles .......................38
Lougenbeel, Major Pinkney .............13
Lueg, Henry .........................65
Lyon's Ferry ....................65, 68, 69

Manresa Grotto ......................13
Marycliff High School .................56
Masonic Temple ......................42
Masterson's Boarding House .........36, 38
Matheny, Jasper ..................37, 47
Maxwell Photographers .................48
Maxwell, William .....................61

McClellan, Capt. George B. ...........
McDonald, Finan ....................
Meyers Falls ......................12,
Meyers, L.W. ......................
Milner Corporation ..................
Milwaukee Railroad ..................
Missions:
    Sacred Heart (Cataldo) .....2, 23, 28, 29,
    St. Francis Regis ..............
    St. Michael's ............17, 18, 33,
    St. Paul's ..................12, 13,
    Tshimakain ..............12, 14, 16,
Monaghan, Ensign John R. .........36, 42,
Monaghan, James ..............16, 29,
Monroe Street Bridge .........34, 36, 41,
Monroe Street Power Plant ...........36,
Moore, F. Rockwood ................
Moran Prairie ......................67,
Mother Joseph ....................
Mt. St. Michael's Cemetery ..........17,
Mt. St. Michael's Scholasticate ......
Myrtle's Peak ....................
Mullan, Lt. John .............23, 28, 69,
Mullan Road .........19-23, 27-29, 65, 68-
Mullan Statue ...................27,
Mullan Tree ....................
Mullouin, Maxim ..................
Murphey, Alonzo ..................
Museums:
    Cheney Cowles ..............43, 49,
    Chewelah ....................
    Lincoln County ..............
    Native American Culture .........19,
    North Idaho ..................
    Wallace Mining ..............

Nash, Home of Judge ..............
Newlon, Thomas ..................
Nix, William ....................
North Idaho College ..............
North West Fur Company ..........10,
Northern Pacific Railroad ......11, 37, 59,

Occident School ..................
Officers' Home, 1878 ............27,
Our Lady of Lourdes Cathedral .....36, 42,
Owhi, Chief ....................

Pacific Fur Company ..............
Palouse Highway ..................
Paradise Prairie ..................
Parks:
    Bowl and Pitcher ..............
    Cannon Hill ..................
    Cliff ......................

orbin ............................... 62
owley ......................... 34, 41, 58
awford State Park ................. 13
rst in Spokane .................... 53
igh Bridge ..................... 33, 34
atatorium ..................... 38, 60
'd Mission (Cataldo) ......... 2, 23, 28, 29
ante's Ferry ............. 17, 19, 20, 21, 23
verfront ...................... 38, 39
verside State .................. 10, 73
son, Robert B. .................. 55
sen, August .................... 29
en Medical Building ............. 45
eful Valley .............. 19, 33, 34, 41
er, Jerome ...................... 63
ington Hotel ................. 36, 44
e, Chief .................... 18, 19
e Prairie ...................... 18
t, Caroline .................... 61
t, William .................. 50, 61
n Building ................... 45
n, Col. Isaac N. ............. 45
h, Franz ..................... 34
ey City ............. 12, 13, 68, 69
er Block ..................... 48
e, Antoine .................. 19, 20
e's Ferry ........ 17, 19, 20, 21, 23, 68
kin, Chief ................... 18
Falls ....................... 27
Frederick ............... 27, 40, 42
Street Bridge ............... 40
ty Flats .................... 34
er Magazine, Old ............ 28
yterian Church, First ......... 43
Home ....................... 62
e, Herman ................... 45
id Peak ..................... 24

han, Chief .................. 24

li, Father Anthony ............ 28
House ...................... 52
v Tower, The .............. 36, 43
, R.N. Mansion .......... 17, 19
rds, Henry ................. 50
rds, J.P.M. ................ 50
ck Drive ................... 61
e, W.A. .................... 60
ts, E.J. .................... 51
Alexander ................. 9, 10
ark Addition ............... 67
ord, Richard Lee ........... 29
, Joe "Kentuck" ............ 71
House ...................... 50
Parkway ............... 9, 50, 61

Rutter, R.L. .......................... 50

St. Aloysius Church ..................63
St. David's Episcopal Church ..............62
St. George's School .....................61
St. John's Cathedral ...................58
St. Joseph's Tridentine Church ...........19
Sacred Heart Hospital .................58
Saltese Lake ..........................64
Sartori Building .......................43
Savoy Hotel ..........................46
Sawmill, Scranton's & Downing's ......36, 39, 41
Scranton, Seth .....................37, 41
Schnebley's Bridge ....................23
Schoenberg, Rev. Wilfred ...........19, 63
Selheim Springs ......................62
Seltice, Chief Andrew ..............27, 64
Seneacquoteen Crossing .........9, 10, 71
Seneacquoteen Trail .............8, 9, 11
Sheridan, Gen. P.M. .................29, 70
Sherman, Gen. William Tecumseh . 26, 28, 29, 70
Sierra Mine Tour ....................29
Sister Joseph Arimathea .............58
Slocum, T.M. .........................72
Smyth's Ford ......................24, 68
Spanish-American War Monument .........59
Spokan Garry .......................9, 35
Spokan Garry's Farm ...............17, 19
Spokan Garry's Grave ...............33, 35
Spokan Garry's Last Homesite ........33, 34
Spokan Garry's School ............8, 9, 14
Spokane & Eastern Trust Bank ...........50
Spokane Bridge .............16, 23, 29, 30,
65, 68, 70-72
Spokane Club ....................36, 42
Spokane County Court-House ...........60
Spokane Falls-Colville Road ...........73
Spokane Falls Review ..................43
Spokane Falls School District ...........58
Spokane House ..........8, 9, 10, 11, 15, 69
Spokane Methodist College ............60
Spokane River ................9, 10, 11, 13,
16, 19, 20, 23, 26, 29, 30, 32, 64, 69
Spring Flat ..........................34
Spring Hill ...........................9
Stafford, Jim ........................67
Steamboats ..........................28
Steptoe Battlefield ................22, 24
Steptoe Butte ....................24, 25
Steptoe, Colonel Edward J. .......24, 25, 35
Stevens, Governor Isaac .........11, 18, 24
Strahorn, Robert .....................51
Street Car Tracks .....................59
Sutton's Red Barn .....................66
Sweeny, Charles .......................47

Terry, W.J. ........................16
Territorial, Old Road ..........59, 68, 72, 73
Texas Road ......................68, 72
Thompson, David ...................13, 72
Thompson, Jesse ......................72
Traders National Bank ...............29, 52
Treaty Rock .........................27
Treaty Tree ......................17, 18
Tridentine Latin Rite Catholic Church ......19
Tshimakain Mission ............12, 14, 16, 69
Tull, F.M. ............................45
Turnbull National Wildlife Refuge .......66, 70

Union Park .........................67
Union Pacific Railroad ..........34, 48, 64, 71
Unitarian Church .....................55
Unusual Windows .....................60

Van Valkenburg Block ..............45, 52
Vinegar Flat .........................67

Waikiki Retreat House ................62
Wakefield, William J.C. ................52
Walker, Mary Richardson ........14, 15, 16, 69
Walker, Reverend Elkanah ............14, 69
Warren, Marshal Joel ..................46
Washington Brick & Lime ............58, 60

Washington Mutual Bank ................
Washington Water Power Company ..14, 16, ?
    36, 39, 41, 64, 66, 67
Washington Water Power Substation .....40,
Water Main Bridge ....................
Water Pumping Plant .............36, 39,
Watering Trough .....................
Welch, Patrick ......................
West Greenwood Cemetery ..............
West 908 Frederick St. ................
Westminster Congregational Church ......50.
White, Aubrey L. ...................51,
White Bluffs Road ...............59, 68,
White Parkway ......................
Whitman Massacre ....................
Whitworth College ...................
Wild Horse Trail ....................
Willis, Mary P. .....................
Willow Springs .....................
Wilson Block .......................
Windsor Hotel ......................37
Witherspoon, A.W. ..................
Wolfe's Lunch Counter ...............
Wooden Warehouse ...................
Woodward, Dorothy E. ...............
Wright, Colonel George ..........13, 23
    29-31, 35, 69

80

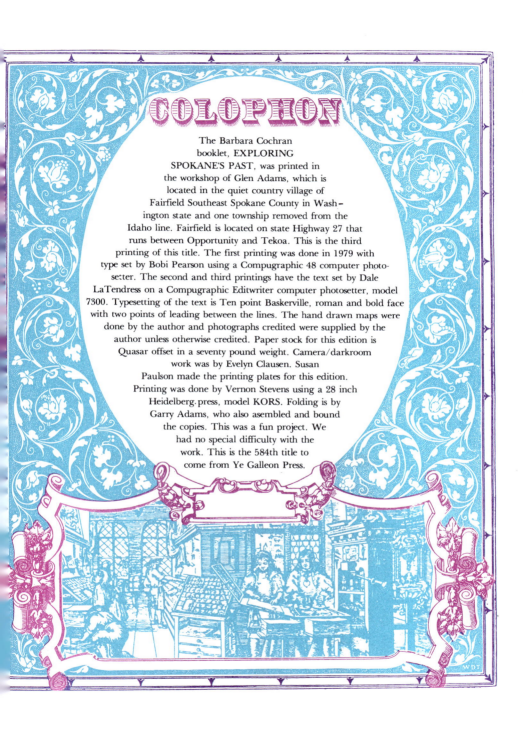

# COLOPHON

The Barbara Cochran
booklet, EXPLORING
SPOKANE'S PAST, was printed in
the workshop of Glen Adams, which is
located in the quiet country village of
Fairfield Southeast Spokane County in Wash–
ington state and one township removed from the
Idaho line. Fairfield is located on state Highway 27 that
runs between Opportunity and Tekoa. This is the third
printing of this title. The first printing was done in 1979 with
type set by Bobi Pearson using a Compugraphic 48 computer photosetter. The second and third printings have the text set by Dale
LaTendress on a Compugraphic Editwriter computer photosetter, model
7300. Typesetting of the text is Ten point Baskerville, roman and bold face
with two points of leading between the lines. The hand drawn maps were
done by the author and photographs credited were supplied by the
author unless otherwise credited. Paper stock for this edition is
Quasar offset in a seventy pound weight. Camera/darkroom
work was by Evelyn Clausen. Susan
Paulson made the printing plates for this edition.
Printing was done by Vernon Stevens using a 28 inch
Heidelberg. press, model KORS. Folding is by
Garry Adams, who also asembled and bound
the copies. This was a fun project. We
had no special difficulty with the
work. This is the 584th title to
come from Ye Galleon Press.